STEINBECK COUNTRY

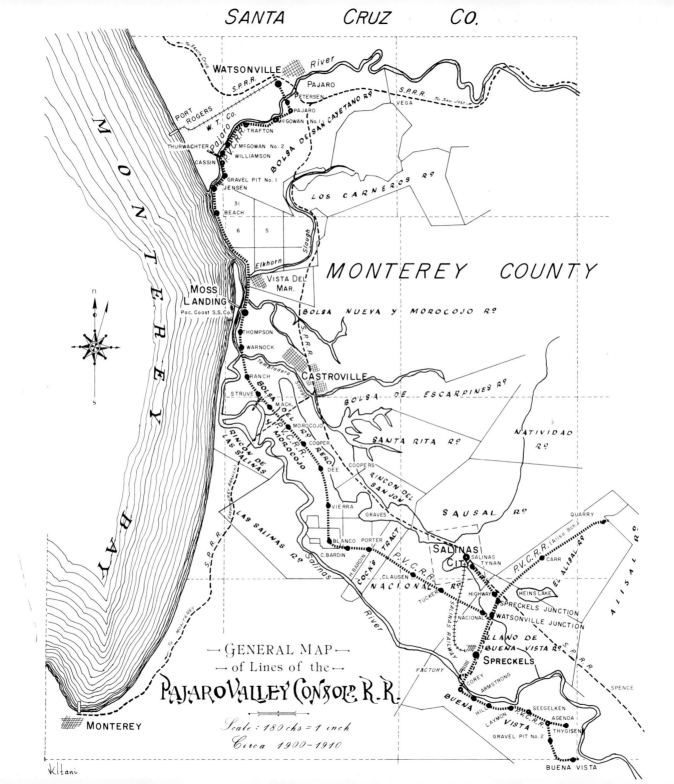

SANTA CRUZ CO.

MONTEREY COUNTY

MONTEREY BAY

WATSONVILLE

CASTROVILLE

SALINAS CITY

SPRECKELS

BUENA VISTA

MONTEREY

—GENERAL MAP—
—of Lines of the—
PAJARO VALLEY CONSOL. R.R.
Scale: 180 chs = 1 inch
Circa 1900-1910

K.Itani

STEINBECK COUNTRY
NARROW GAUGE

Horace W. Fabing and Rick Hamman

PRUETT PUBLISHING COMPANY
Boulder, Colorado

EB

First Edition
1 2 3 4 5 6 7 8 9

Printed in the United States of America

Library of Congress Cataloging-in-Publication Data

Fabing, Horace W.
   Steinbeck country narrow gauge.

   Bibliography: p.
   Includes index.
   1. Pajaro Valley Consolidated Railroad.
2. Railroads--California--Salinas River Valley.
3. Salinas River Valley (Calif.)--History.
I. Hamman, Rick, 1944-   . II. Title.
TF25.P25F33   1985   385'.52'0979476   85-16776
ISBN 0-87108-693-X

4-10-86

Steinbeck Country Narrow Gauge

About the title: At first glance it sounds a bit pretentious on our part to use such a well-known author's name in the title of a book primarily on narrow gauge railroads of the Pajaro and Salinas valleys. On closer examination, however, it is both concise and just.

John Ernst Steinbeck was born to Olive and John Steinbeck on February 27, 1902, in Salinas, California. John's father, John Ernst Steinbeck Sr., was well entrenched in the local area and was for many years the treasurer of Monterey County. John's mother, Olive, was a school teacher in the local Salinas Valley public school system. Together, they provided the base for John's understanding and inquisitiveness which would later lead to his many powerful short stories and novels.

During John's formative years in Salinas the Pajaro Valley Consolidated Railroad was at its prime, and the Spreckels Sugar Company was a mainstay of the community. During his high school days he worked in the fields, on the nearby cattle ranches, and for the Spreckels Sugar Company. Over a period of six years, after graduating from high school in 1919, and while attending Stanford University, he worked as an assistant chemist at the Spreckels Sugar Company factory in Spreckels and later as a night chemist at the Manteca facility. From this early background came many of the characters and settings for his books.

As John Steinbeck matured and became Steinbeck the writer, works such as *East of Eden, The Red Pony, Tortilla Flats, Of Mice and Men, Cannery Row,* and *The Pastures of Heaven* flowed from his pen describing the life and times of an area that today is simply referred to as Steinbeck Country.

Thus, rather than trying to call this book something like the Pajaro Valley Consolidated Narrow Gauge or the Narrow Gauge Railroads of the Pajaro & Salinas valleys, we have called it what it is: *Steinbeck Country Narrow Gauge.*

CONTENTS

PREFACE

THIS BOOK IS PRIMARILY ABOUT a quality little California narrow gauge railroad that quietly operated for thirty-five very successful years in the lush agricultural regions of the Pajaro and Salinas valleys and along the shoreline of Monterey Bay. Not much has been written about this pristine little slim line, because it operated over fifty years ago in an area that had a population base of less than 5,000 people. It was a privately held concern, essentially serving the needs of its parent owner, the Spreckels Sugar Company, and it didn't get much day to day attention. It had no great mountains to scale, it crossed no major trestles or bridges of any height, it traversed no tunnel bores of any length, it saw no serious fluctuations in weather patterns, and it served no metropolises of any stature.

The name of this relatively unknown narrow gauge was the Pajaro Valley Consolidated Railroad. It started out in 1890 as the brainchild of Claus Spreckels, the well-known California and Hawaiian Sugar King, who wanted to ship raw sugar and finished product from his Watsonville factory to his San Francisco plant for final refinement and distribution without having to pay the steep freight rates of the local Southern Pacific operations. To accomplish this goal he simply built a little narrow gauge road, then the Pajaro Valley Railroad, from his Watsonville factory to the Pacific Coast Steamship Company port at Moss Landing on Monterey Bay. In short order he was able to competitively ship sugar via a rail-ship connection to his San Francisco facility without the services of the Southern Pacific.

In time this Claus Spreckels narrow gauge was extended farther and farther into the Salinas Valley until finally it reached the outskirts of Salinas itself. This caused an increase in freight unrelated to the sugar factory and passenger traffic from the local farming areas to the cities of Salinas and Watsonville and to the seaport connection provided by the Pacific Coast Steamship Company at Moss Landing.

From raw to finished product by rail—over 90 years of continuous operation in the Steinbeck Country—Spreckels Sugar, Spreckels, California. Photograph by Rick Hamman

By 1897, Claus Spreckels's enterprises had expanded so much that he built the largest sugar refinery in the world near Salinas, at a location to be known as Spreckels. With the opening of the factory in 1900, the ever-burgeoning railroad became the Pajaro Valley Consolidated. Soon after, the road was extended even farther, with fifteen miles of additional branch lines being built to Salinas, Alisal, and Buena Vista. Altogether, by 1908 the perky little "P-Vine" was operating daily passenger and freight service over forty-three miles of mainline and branch line tracks.

This day-to-day reputable operation continued, basically unchanged, until well into the late 1920s, when the arrival of the automobile, bus, and truck on the scene and the coming depression spelled the end of the Pajaro Valley Consolidated.

This then is the story of the gallant little PVC and of the other local standard and narrow gauge railroads that came before, during, and after its lifespan. Also, this is the intertwining story of the Spreckels Sugar Company and of the Pacific Coast Steamship Company and how they, in conjunction with the railroads, came together to help mold and shape the turn-of-the-century history of Steinbeck Country.

As we complete this book we would like to reserve this space to graciously thank a number of organizations and individuals who were responsible for providing the necessary research, information, resources, maps, photographs, drawings, and other facts and artifacts that helped bring this book into being. They are:

Organizations

Amstar Corporation
Williams, Dimond Company
Stanford University Libraries
University of California at Berkeley (Bancroft Library)
University of California at Santa Cruz (Special Collections)
California State Library at Sacramento
Monterey Library
Monterey County Library, Salinas
Salinas Library
Watsonville Library
California State Public Utilities Commission
United States Geological Survey, Menlo Park
Society of California Pioneers
Santa Cruz County Clerks Office
Monterey County Clerks Office
Pajaro Valley Historical Association
Monterey County Historical Society

Individuals

Steven Abbott

Morris Casanelli

Alvin Graves

William Lehman

Earl Power

Fred Stoes

Guy Dunscomb

Marc Tunzi

Charles Vierra

Viola Gockel

Bruce Anderson

Mrs. Carrie Hansen

Carl Gatske

Bruce MacGregor

James Ross Riley

Vernon Sappers

Benny Romano

Donald Whiteman

John Weiner

Dorothy Asbury

John Hughes

Francis Guido

Paul Pioda

William H. Anderson

Miss Rose Rhyner

Edward Pfingst

Albert Vierra

Ted Wurm

Jerry McCabe

A special vote of appreciation goes to Tom Ryan of Amstar who gave us carte blanche use of the Spreckels Sugar Company collection of photographs, drawings, and maps and who personally devoted a considerable amount of his time to this project; to Vic Itani, once again thank you for your fine map work; to Fred Rosche, your special copy camera proved invaluable; and finally, to our wives, Nan Fabing and Carol Hamman, and our respective families for tolerating the pursuit of railroad history.

Horace W. Fabing
Rick Hamman

I / STEINBECK COUNTRY

Before there were Railroads

BEFORE THE COMING OF MAN and the various forms of transportation he would use to move himself and his goods from one place to another, there was the central coast land of California. Then it was primarily a plain through which the drainage of the Great Interior Valley and the Salinas Valley passed on its way to Monterey Bay and the Pacific Ocean. As time progressed and glaciation, volcanic activity, upward movement, and erosion took place, the various local valleys were formed, bounded by the Santa Cruz Range, the Gabilan Range, and the Santa Lucia Mountains. Eventually the interior valley was cut off from the coastal area of Monterey Bay, and the once-great course of water that had helped to create the Pajaro Valley became a much milder stream. Today that stream, the Pajaro River, finds its origins in the San Juan, Santa Clara, and San Benito valleys.

Unlike the Pajaro River, the Salinas River remains a somewhat larger watercourse. It begins in the mountains northeast of San Luis Obispo and the southern Santa Lucias, where it is mixed with the Nacimento and San Antonio rivers and then flows for about eighty miles northwest to Monterey Bay. Over the years it has formed a valley which has about 640,000 acres of prime bottom land and is over fifteen miles wide at its mouth. Additionally, because of previous shale and other sedimentary rock formations overlaid by a rich soil deposit, the Salinas remains the largest underground river in the United States. This, coupled with heavy amounts of rainfall from Pacific Coast storms that sweep over the Santa Lucia Mountains, has helped to create what many call the "Valley of the Nile" or more recently, the "Salad Bowl of America."

Even today, though most external signs of a previous time are no longer visible, an underwater canyon can be found starting at the joint outpouring of the Pajaro and Salinas rivers and extending several miles out to sea, to a depth of over 10,000 feet.

It is early in the 1870s at Captain Moss's Landing. A flat-bottom boat, or lighter, sits beached on the Salinas River bank, Island side. Off in the distance people stop what they are doing to watch the photographer take this picture. Photograph courtesy Pajaro Valley Historical Association

Before the land became known as Steinbeck Country, or the Pajaro and Salinas valleys, or the Monterey Bay Area, or any of the many other names the early Spanish explorers bestowed upon it, the Indian had already lived on it, and had had names for it, for at least 12,000 years, and possibly as long as 40,000 years.

The first white man in the New World to describe these Central Coast Indians and their land was General Sebastian Viscayno of Spain in 1602. He had been sent by the Count of Monterey to explore the western coast of California for possible future occupation. Eventually he and his squadron anchored in a sheltered cove southeast of a protective point. The cove was later named the Port of Monterey, after the count, and the point was named Point Pinos, after some nearby pine trees.

In time more Spanish explorers, like Don Gaspar de Portola in 1769, came to establish presidios and secure the land for Spain. Shortly thereafter the padres, under Father Junipero Serra, began their famed mission system, the Indians learned to work and live in the Spanish culture, and the beginnings of a new society in upper, or "Alta," California took shape.

By 1800, Alta California was well on the way to colonization, and the first Spanish land grant of 8,000 plus acres in Steinbeck Country had been granted to a retired soldier, José Soberanes. Within the span of forty more years twenty-seven other large grants were given, and farming and cattle raising became the prime businesses of the Pajaro and Salinas valleys.

By 1849 Steinbeck Country had seen the end of Spanish rule, separation from Mexican control, and a new government formed under the American flag. It was also about this time that gold was officially discovered. Thousands of people came west in search of it, and the very next year California became a state with Monterey as its capital. Thus began the real habitation of the lands surrounding Monterey Bay, the valleys of the Salinas, the Pajaro, and the San Lorenzo rivers, and the cities of Monterey and Santa Cruz.

During the next ten years the population of the new state of California expanded from less than 200 non-Indian inhabitants to over 80,000 permanent residents. With this expansion came many farmers and ranchers, crafts- and tradespeople, looking for a new future in a new land. For Santa Cruz and Monterey counties, and particularly for the Pajaro and Salinas valleys, this meant many new squatters and settlers coming to get their 160 acres of government land. Soon already established town centers around Monterey Bay became respectable communities. There was Monterey itself, now a well-known West Coast seaport; the thriving city of Santa Cruz, across the bay to the north, at the mouth of the San Lorenzo River; and Watsonville, the commercial center of the Pajaro Valley.

One should not come away with the mistaken notion that people arriving in the Steinbeck Country of the 1850s were well on the way to acquiring a good piece of previously uninhabited bottom land. Of prime importance was the fact that most of the land in the Pajaro and Salinas valleys, previously held by Mexico and sold to the United States, was owned by local rancheros. They had broken away from Mexican rule only to be taken over a short time later by the American government when young Lieutenant Fremont arrived on the scene. Thus, the original Californians and those who arrived later had many problems to solve, including land ownership, clear title, homesteading, and community relationships.

As the land of the Pajaro and Salinas valleys continued to be developed through the 1860s, small communities began to appear at crossroads and other highly trafficked areas. The first such community to be established in the Salinas Valley was Castroville, in 1864, by Juan B. Castro on the Bolsa Nueva Y Moro Cojo Rancho. Shortly thereafter, at the Los Angeles–San Francisco–Monterey stage interchange point, the town of Salinas City came into being. It was here that an inn, run by Carlisle S. Abbott, had existed for many years to meet the needs of the weary traveler and, little by little, other buildings had gone up in the mustard fields around it. In time Salinas City came to be the center of activity in the Salinas Valley. The Monterey County Court House was moved there, and Esquire Abbott was one of the town's more prominent citizens. And nine miles south of Salinas City David Jacks started developing the community of Chular on the old Rancho Chular,

Lumber schooners at the Moss Landing wharf, circa 1875. Photograph courtesy Monterey County Historical Society

which he had confiscated years before.

Of all the cast of characters who influenced the course of history in Steinbeck Country during its formative years, perhaps the name that belongs at the top of the list is David Jacks. David Jacks, the money lender, started his career by lending much-needed cash to the larger local landowners against deeds of trust at the rate of two percent per month for two years. If they could not pay, he picked up the note. As his business dealings expanded, he began paying delinquent taxes on property negligent Spanish and Mexican rancheros had failed to pay, without telling them. He then approached them at a later date requesting they pay the taxes plus his interest or turn over the deed. As he acquired more and more large parcels of land in this manner he then rented them out to worthy tenant farmers at the rate of half their profits after costs. In another ingenious move he took all the vagrants out of the county jails and off the tax-supported rolls by agreeing to feed and house them in return for free labor.

During the early 1860s David Jacks acquired title to most of the tidelands from the outskirts of the City of Monterey to the mouth of the Salinas River. This included a seemingly worthless two-mile strip of very narrow sandy peninsula running between Monterey Bay and the Salinas River. On the eastern bank of the river, across from the peninsula, were the Moro Cojo (Lame Moor) and Elkhorn slough entrances. The sloughs connecting with the Salinas River and protected by the peninsula all came together to form a small natural inland harbor. In a very short time this worthless area gained the attention of many profit-seeking individuals.

The first person to try to take advantage of the commercial potential of this harbor had been the Frenchman Paul Lazere, who, in the late 1850s, had subdivided 300 acres of land into saleable city lots, all within the boundaries of the community he named St. Paul. While his ill-conceived and poorly laid-out plans would shortly end in failure, he was responsible for establishing both a salt works on, and a ferry across, the Elkhorn (originally Elk Horn) Slough.

In April of 1866 Captain Charles Moss, with his wife and two sons, settled on a small farm about a mile from the harbor. Because of his political and philosophical views he had come to California seeking refuge and had ended up on the coast. As Captain Moss became more and more aware of the area, with its harbor, narrow peninsula, and the gentle tides of Monterey Bay, he soon realized that here would be a spot where ships could be loaded. In short order he enlisted the services of some small boats, built a warehouse on the peninsula, and started loading local grain onto coastal ships. At first the grain had to be carried by manpower out through the waves to waiting surf boats beyond the breakers and then rowed to the ships anchored a short distance offshore. By July of the same year, however, a 200-foot wharf had been constructed and the boats began loading from the dock. In no time at all the word on the coast was that things were happening at Moss's Landing.

In addition to Moss's Landing there was the Port of Watsonville, established by captains Brennan and Sudden in the 1850s, far up Elkhorn Slough, less than a mile from the center of town. From the port, also known as Brennan's Landing, the perky little steamer *Salinas*, and others like her, made scheduled trips for over twenty years to the various ports on Monterey Bay and back and forth to San Francisco.

A short time after the arrival of Captain Moss, yet another seafaring captain, Cato Vierra, happened on the scene and took over Paul Lazere's salt works and the Elkhorn Slough ferry. Vierra, at Moss's urging, together with several others, started operating lighters (flat-bottom boats) on the local sloughs to transport grain to Moss's warehouse on the peninsula for transport by larger, deepwater ships. During this particular time conditions were such that lighters could navigate up the Elkhorn Slough as far as Hudson's, Miller's, and Brennan's landings and for a considerable distance along the Moro Cojo and Tembladero sloughs towards Salinas.

As the ex-captains' local enterprises continued to prosper, significant changes began to take place at the harbor. First, Vierra built a bridge across the Salinas River to the peninsula so that horsedrawn wagons could unload at Moss's warehouse or on the wharf. Second, the wharf, now known as Moss

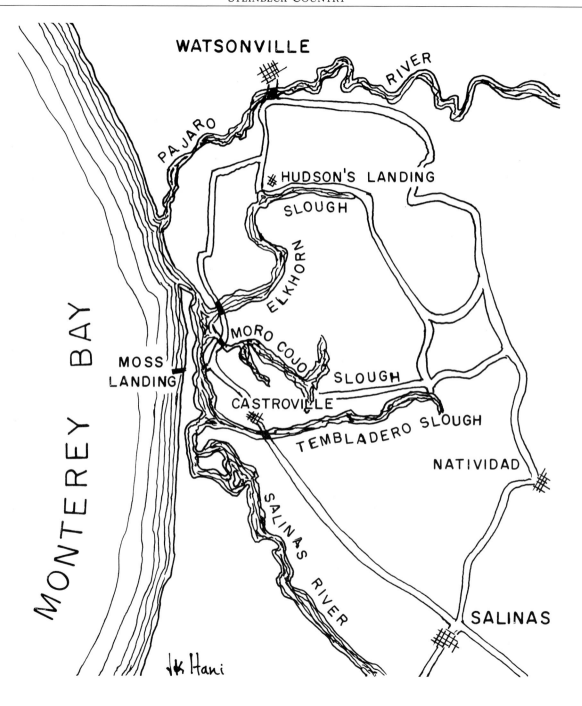

MONTEREY BAY

WATSONVILLE

PAJARO RIVER

HUDSON'S LANDING

SLOUGH

ELKHORN

MORO COJO

SLOUGH

MOSS LANDING

CASTROVILLE

TEMBLADERO SLOUGH

NATIVIDAD

SALINAS RIVER

SALINAS

JK Hani

Landing, was extended much farther into the bay so that steamers and schooners could tie up for direct transshipment of freight. Next, Moss built additional warehouses on the peninsula to allow for an expanded storage capacity of 15,000 tons of grain. Finally, because of the peninsula's topography, coupled with its being separated from the mainland by the Salinas River, it soon became known as "the Island," a name it has retained to the present day. Thus, by 1871 the captains had turned the harbor into a thriving freight and passenger center where many coastal ships were seen loading and off-loading their precious cargos and traveling patrons.

Just about the time all seemed to be going so well, David Jacks took note of the success Charles Moss was having on his peninsula and demanded $10,000 for the land beneath Moss's warehouse and wharf facilities. Moss had unknowingly assumed the sandspit belonged to no one. Jacks had supposedly received the land from the City of Monterey as part payment for legal work he had performed for its benefit. Jacks had never had clear title to the property, but the City of Monterey had accepted from him a property tax payment on the land. As the land was miles from the city proper, Monterey did not choose to contest Jacks's claim on the Island. As a result, it was many years before Moss and Jacks finally came to a private settlement.

When the Railroads Came

Adam stopped in New York long enough to buy clothes for himself and Cathy before they climbed on the train which bore them across the continent. How they happened to go to the Salinas Valley is very easy to understand.

In that day the railroads – growing, fighting among themselves, striving to increase and to dominate – used every means to increase their traffic. The companies not only advertised in the newspapers, they issued booklets and broadsides describing and picturing the beauty and richness of the West. No claim was too extravagant – wealth was unlimited. The Southern Pacific Railroad, headed by the wild energy of Leland Stanford, had begun to dominate the Pacific Coast not only in transportation but in politics. Its rails extended down the valleys. New towns sprang up, new sections were opened and populated, for the company had to create customers to get custom.

The long Salinas Valley was part of the exploitation. Adam had seen and studied a fine color broadside which set forth the valley as that region which heaven unsuccessfully imitated. After reading the literature, anyone who did not want to settle in the Salinas Valley was crazy.

East of Eden
John Steinbeck, 1952

As time progressed and Steinbeck Country became an established agricultural and livestock area, the call went out for better forms of transportation to meet the needs of the many expanding communities. The cities of San Francisco and San Jose had completed a rail line between themselves in 1864, and talk was that another company, the Southern Pacific, was going to take that line over, extend it on down the Santa Clara Valley to Gilroy and Hollister, through the mountains into the San Joaquin Valley, and then on to the Atlantic & Pacific Railroad at the Colorado River. If such a line were completed, it wouldn't take much to bring a branch line from the Pajaro and Salinas valleys to Gilroy.

The Central Pacific, however, building east out of Sacramento toward the Union Pacific, which in turn was building west, was not about to let a second transcontinental railroad establish a foothold in California. Consequently, they purchased controlling interest in the Southern Pacific and delayed the SP's connection with the A&P. By 1868, the Central Pacific had devised new plans for the SP and started out from San Jose under the name of the Santa Clara & Pajaro Valley to build a connecting line with the Texas & Pacific, the A&P's competition across the south. By 1869, the line had reached Gilroy and was headed for Hollister and Tres Pinos. In 1870, they publicly incorporated all their interests under the Southern Pacific–Central Pacific Big Four banner and divested any ties to the Atlantic & Pacific.

Unknown to the local people of the Pajaro and Salinas valleys, who saw their only possible rail connection heading south down the adjoining valley, the Southern Pacific was now at odds with the Atlantic & Pacific. As a result, the Atlantic & Pacific was considering building to San Francisco by themselves, over the Tehachapis, across the San Joaquin Valley, through the mountains to Paso Robles, up the Salinas Valley, north past Watsonville and Santa Cruz, and along the coast. In an effort to block such an operation, and at the same time open up the rich Steinbeck Country lands, the Southern Pacific held ground-breaking ceremonies in Gilroy on July 17, 1871, and began a forty-five-mile branch line toward Watsonville and Salinas City.

As the SP branch was projected, it left Gilroy traveling south until it reached the Pajaro River. From there it followed the river's winding course west through the narrow Pajaro Gap, between the Santa Cruz and Gabilan mountains, and then on to the Pajaro Valley itself. Initially, the local citizens of Watsonville were incensed because the SP right-of-way remained on the south side of the Pajaro River after its crossing in the Pajaro Gap. This meant that rather than coming through Watsonville proper, the railroad was actually going to stop just across the river at a spot they would call Pajaro, later Watsonville Junction. From Pajaro the line, when finished, would continue on across the slough lands of the Moro Cojo and into Castroville, finally reaching Salinas City. It had been the SP's original intention to build a roundhouse and yard facility at Castroville, but when old Juan B. Castro started jacking up the price on the land, the railroad moved on to Salinas City with its construction plans.

On November 26, 1871, the Southern Pacific began service from Watsonville (Pajaro) to San Francisco, and the Pajaro Valley was connected to the markets of the world. On November 1 of the following year Salinas City saw service begin, and all of Steinbeck Country took one giant step forward into the era of progress, productivity, and commerce.

Having the large financial influence in the local area that he did, it didn't take very long for David Jacks to convince the SP brass to extend their line to his Rancho Chular and beyond to Soledad. By August of 1873 the Salinas Branch was complete, and standard gauge, high speed, mainline freight and

289 SOUTHERN PACIFIC R. R. OF CALIFORNIA.

CHARLES CROCKER, President,
DAVID D. COLTON, Vice-President.
E. H. MILLER, Jr., Treasurer.
J. L. WILLCUTT, Secretary and
Gen. Passenger and Ticket Agent.
CHARLES J. ROBINSON, Auditor.
N. T. SMITH, Cashier.
C. P. HUNTINGTON, Agt. and Atty.,
No. 9 Nassau Street, New York.

A. C. BASSETT, Superintendent
and Freight Agt., North. Div.,
San Francisco, Cal.
E. E. HEWITT, Supt. Los Angeles
Division, Los Angeles, Cal.
C. F. SMURR, Fht.Agt.Los Angeles
Division, Los Angeles, Cal.
General Offices—San Francisco, Cal.

NORTHERN DIVISION.

Pas.	Pas.	Pas.	Mls	May 22, 1876.	Mls	Pas.	Pas.	Pas.
P.M.	P.M.	A.M.		(San Francisco time.)		A.M.	A.M.	P.M.
*4 40	+3 25	*8 30	0	lv..San Francisco..ar.	143	8 50	10 00	5 35
5 00	3 46	8 53	4	......Bernal......	139	8 29	...	5 15
5 07	3 52	8 59	6	....San Miguel.....	137	8 22	9 37	5 07
5 21	4 06	9 14	12	......Baden........	131	8 06	9 25	4 48
5 26	...	9 20	14	.....San Bruno.....	129	8 00	9 20	4 40
5 34	4 16	9 27	17	......Millbrae.....	126	7 53	9 14	4 30
5 45	4 27	9 40	21	.....San Mateo.....	122	7 42	9 05	4 15
5 55	4 35	9 51	25	......Belmont......	118	7 32	8 56	4 05
6 03	4 43	10 01	28	....Redwood City....	115	7 23	8 48	3 55
6 15	4 53	10 13	33	....Menlo Park....	110	7 11	8 38	3 43
6 22	4 59	10 21	35	......Mayfield......	108	7 04	8 31	3 34
6 32	5 08	10 32	38	...Mountain View...	105	6 54	8 22	3 20
6 39	...	10 42	41	......Murphy's......	102	6 48	...	3 11
6 45	...	10 48	44	.....Lawrence's.....	99	6 43	...	3 05
6 53	5 25	10 59	47	....Santa Clara....	96	6 36	8 06	2 54
7 00	5 31	11 12	50	......San Jose.....	93	*6 30	8 00	2 45
P.M.	6 01	11 46	63	......Coyote......	80	A.M.	7 28	2 04
	6 07	11 54	66	......Perry's......	77		7 21	1 56
	6 21	12 13	73	......Tennant......	70		7 07	1 38
	6 37	12 48	80	......Gilroy.......	63		6 52	1 18
P.M.	P.M.			LEAVE] [ARRIVE		A.M.	NO'N	
+6 47	*1 25		80	......Gilroy......	20	6 40	12 25	
7 39	2 15		94	......Hollister......	6	5 50	11 35	
8 00	2 40		100	....Trespinos.....	0	+5 30	11 15	
P.M.	P.M.			ARRIVE] [LEAVE		A.M.	§A.M	
6 51	12 56		83	...Carnadero....	60	6 38	12 56	
7 23	1 07		86	......Sargent's......	57	6 06	12 43	
7 30	1 37		96	........Vega........	47	+6 00	12 09	
P.M.	1 45		99	......Pajaro......	43	A.M.	12 01	
	2 15		110	.....Castroville.....	33		11 30	
	2 47		118	......Salinas......	25		11 10	
	3 32		128	......Chualar.......	14		10 20	
	3 55		134	.....Gonzales......	8		10 00	
	4 25		143	.....Soledad......	0		*9 35	
	P.M.			ARRIVE] [LEAVE			A.M.	

* Daily; + daily, except Sunday; § Sunday only.

Typical of the early Southern Pacific trains operating into Steinbeck Country was this short charmer at Pajaro, later Watsonville Junction. Photograph courtesy Pajaro Valley Historical Association

The year is 1875. The Southern Pacific standard gauge has arrived in Salinas City, and judging from this scene, they are here to stay. Photograph courtesy Monterey County Historical Society

passenger service had become a taken-for-granted reality between the San Francisco Bay Area and Steinbeck Country.

With the arrival of the railroad it was the beginning of the end for traffic on the sloughs and small sailing ships out of Moss Landing. Barges continued to ply Elkhorn Slough for several more years, but a land reclamation project dam was built across the Moro Cojo Slough, ending its use. A small number of wagons continued to deliver grain to the warehouses for storage and shipment to protest the service and rates of the Southern Pacific, but with a continuing decline in shipping freight by water, all could see the writing on the wall. As a result, Captain Moss sold out his interests and moved to Oregon, leaving the fate of Moss Landing to its new owner, the Pacific Coast Steamship Company.

The Monterey & Salinas Valley Railroad

With the arrival of the first SP freight and passenger trains in the Salinas Valley, the local rancheros and farmers looked forward with keen anticipation to the potential for greater production and better distribution of the area's agricultural products. Unfortunately, this anticipation soon turned to disgust when the railroad began taking advantage of its captive customers by raising the freight rates to an unbearable level. To compete with the Southern Pacific, a group of prominent Salinas Valley citizens, led by Carlisle Abbott, who had recently acquired the 16,400-acre San Lorenzo Rancho, began calling for an independently owned and operated railroad to be built from the Port of Monterey to Salinas City and beyond.

Also included in this group of citizens was the money lender Mr. Jacks. Jacks stood to gain from the proposal in two ways. First, he owned most of the lands around the city of Monterey and much of the property between there and Salinas City. Because of poor roads, the ever-changing Salinas River, and the extensive tidelands separating the old Spanish capital from the rest of Steinbeck Country, Monterey had remained a city of only minor importance. With a rail connection to Salinas City, however, Monterey would almost immediately

become a major West Coast seaport, and David Jacks's financial position, based on his local interests, would substantially improve. Second, with such a line having to pass through his lands, he would have direct access to the many coastal ships docking at Monterey.

On February 26, 1874 formal articles of incorporation were filed in the Monterey County Court House in Salinas City for the Monterey & Salinas Valley Railroad. The same articles were filed in Sacramento on March 5. The capital stock of the corporation was put at 3,000 shares with a par value of $100 each, and at the time of incorporation over fifty percent of the shares had already been subscribed to. Among others, David Jacks was listed as holding $25,000 in shares and C.S. Abbott as holding another $20,000 in shares. Officers and directors of the company were: C.S. Abbott, president; David Jacks, treasurer; A. Gonzoles, superintendent and secretary; C.I. Chamberlain, George Pomeroy, S.B. Gordon, and M.E. Gonzoles, directors.

The Monterey & Salinas Valley Railroad was incorporated as a narrow gauge, three feet between the rails, steam railroad to operate from a 1,000-foot wharf at the foot of Washington Street in Monterey to Salinas City. Future expansion plans included building south down the Salinas Valley and north to Watsonville. The length of the initial line when completed would be 18½ miles, it would use thirty-five-pound iron rail, and it would have a maximum ruling grade of 105 feet to the mile.

Earlier, in the spring of 1868, the Monterey and Natividad Railroad had been chartered to build from a Monterey Bay tidewater terminal to Salinas City. The preliminary survey of the projected road was conducted by John F. Kidder, later of Nevada County Narrow Gauge fame. Mr. Kidder was sent by a San Francisco steamship company to survey the line, but evidently it was decided the area was not yet capable of supporting a railroad, as no construction ever took place. Now, six

This early 1870s view reveals a time when both the Southern Pacific and the Monterey & Salinas Valley made connections in Salinas City. Photograph courtesy Rudy Peden Collection

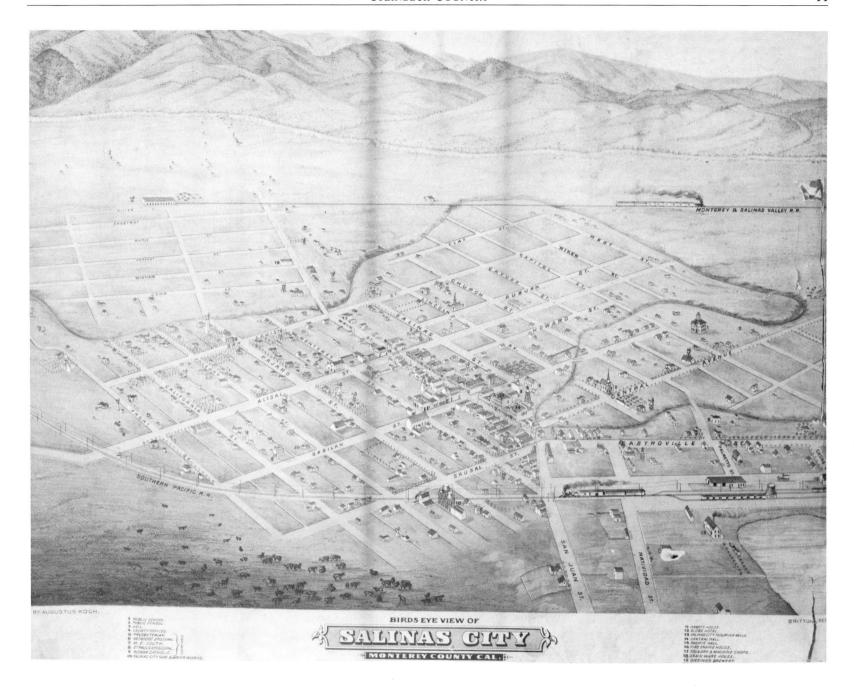

BY AUGUSTUS KOCH.

BIRDS EYE VIEW OF
SALINAS CITY
MONTEREY COUNTY CAL.

BRITTON, REY

years later, Mr. Kidder was retained by the Monterey & Salinas Valley to be its chief engineer during the construction of the new railroad.

Shortly after the ink had dried on the articles of incorporation, Mr. Kidder went to work on the actual surveying of the Monterey & Salinas Valley. As there were to be no tunnels, the only real problem of any consequence was picking a spot to cross the ever-changing bed, with its shifting quicksands, of the Salinas River. To do this Kidder decided on 1,100 feet of wooden trestle along with five 60-foot sections of wooden bridge crossing the channel proper. The right-of-way itself held close to the coast, requiring no substantial changes in elevation and no surmounting of major geographical obstacles. When completed, Mr. Kidder was able to lay out a route containing 14¾ miles of straight track and only 182 degrees or 3¾ miles of gradually curving right-of-way. The longest ascent was a gentle 79 feet per mile over a distance of 2,700 feet, and the steepest grade was only 650 feet long.

The surveying and initial preparation of the line was over in a matter of weeks. On April 20, 1874, official groundbreaking ceremonies were held at a point two miles northeast of Monterey. After the opening speeches were given, the main event of the day began. Although not spectacular by any means, it consisted of President C.S. Abbott demonstrating the use of a revolutionary horsedrawn grader to Engineer Kidder's construction crew of 140 workers, half Caucasian and half Chinese.

With the festivities over, the actual construction got under way. The line as laid out was easy to put down, and all looked forward to beginning operations within six months. Starting at Monterey, the line followed what is now the Southern Pacific to a point north of Marina. From here the line went northeast over the rolling hills to the Salinas River crossing. The river crossing was about two miles south of the present SP Salinas River bridge. From the crossing the road turned southeast in almost a perfect straight line, ending at the Salinas Terminal located at what is now the intersection of Pajaro and Willow streets. By July 23, 1874 the right-of-way was completed to the

river crossing, and by August 29 construction had reached Salinas. By the end of September the Salinas River bridge was completed and service was anticipated shortly.

During the beginning of construction the initial motive power and rolling stock were ordered. From Baldwin would come a classic 2-6-0, 18-ton, narrow gauge Mogul, to be known as locomotive No.1, the *C.S. Abbott,* in honor of the road's president. From Carter Brothers would come forty-two flatcars, eight boxcars, two cabooses, a combination baggage-coach, and a coach. Almost all of the rolling stock was built by Carter Brothers on the property at Monterey.

By October of 1874 the newly completed Monterey Depot and the 50-foot by 400-foot company warehouse, along with the car and blacksmith shops, were ready for use. Over at Salinas City the new warehouse was already bulging with grain, and another 25,000 sacks of like produce sat stacked outside, all awaiting shipment. The C.S. Abbott and all of the rolling stock were on hand. The turntables and water tanks were operational and, in general, the Monterey & Salinas Valley Railroad was about to become a new area resource.

On October 23, 1874, at 8:30 A.M., amid local fanfare and celebration, the first mixed-mail-accommodation train commenced its single roundtrip operations from Monterey to Salinas City over the first narrow gauge railroad to be completed in California. Before the day was over the little narrow gauge Monterey Bay shoreline skimmer had returned to the port with its first load of beans and barley from the J. Bardin Ranch. Thus, the spunky little M&SV had been built entirely with local pride and local capital, and there was hope that the Southern Pacific would no longer be the only freight and passenger game in town.

By November things along the M&SV had settled down to a normal routine. Each day would see engine No.1 and the relatively empty mixed train leaving Monterey at 8:30 in the morning and returning by 3:15 in the afternoon with a healthy consist. Once the train had arrived, direct connections could then be made to the Goodall, Nelson and Perkins Steamship Company on the wharf. On the average, 300 tons of grain per

MONTEREY & SALINAS VALLEY R. R. COMPANY.

Way-Bill No.   of Merchandise forwarded from   Station to

187   Per   Train   o'clock,   M.

Date	No. of Car. W.B.	SHIPPER.	MARK.	CONSIGNEE.	DESCRIPTION OF GOODS.	WEIGHT.	TOTAL WEIGHT.	MEASURE.	TOTAL MEASURE.	RATE.	ADVANCE CHARGES.	RAILROAD FREIGHT.
Mch 10	54 31	F. 76. & P.	Als Ol Smith	2 Bbls Wine		200						
--- 26	55 12	--- ---	1. -- Fenton & C.	5 Bbls Stoves								
				1 Bbl Rims								
				1 -- Bnt Fels								
				1 Set Bxes								
				16 --- Grib								
				7 Springs								
				2 Bxs Skents								
				1 C Cro Drill								
				1 Vise		5650			5 c	9 88	5 66
			35									
Mch 25	55 12	G. N. & P.	-- Otto Dessing	2 Bbls Hops								
				1 Bbl Shovels								
				1 Sk Malt								
				3 " Mdse								
				1 C Faucett		600 6250				1 50	1 50
			5									
Mch 27	56 7	A. Harris	A. P. Hulse	1 Car Lumber		16000				1 25	10 00
--- ---	57 9	---	--- ---	1 --- ---		16000				1 25	10 00
--- ---	58 39	"	" "	1 " "		16000				1 25	10 00
- "	59 67	"	" "	1 " "		16000				1 25	10 00
" "	60 79	"	" "	1 " "		16000				1 25	10 00
- "	61 49	Pch & P	H. Ramsey	36 Bxs Dried Fruit & 4 Bx Shells		500 85000				8 75	5 00

This M&SV Waybill and freight forwarding record indicates that connections were being made with the GN&P (Goodall Nelson and Perkins) ships Kalorama *and* Santa Cruz. *The* Kalorama *was a 545-ton wooden vessel dating back to pre–Civil War days. It was lost at sea March 30, 1877. The* Santa Cruz, *built in 1868, was a similar-size ship of 600 tons that saw service well into the early 1920s. Courtesy Monterey Library*

GOODALL-NELSON-PERKINS

Pacific Coast Steamship Co.

Splendid Steamers leave San Francisco for following

SOUTHERN COAST PORTS

EVERY TWO DAYS:

SANTA CRUZ,   SANTA MONICA,
   MONTEREY,   SAN PEDRO.
      SAN LUIS O'BISPO,   LOS ANGELES,
         PASO DE ROBELS (Hot Springs),   SAN BARNADINO,
            SANTA BARBARA,   ANAHEIM,
               SAN BUENAVENTURA,   SAN DIEGO,
AND ALL POINTS IN SOUTHERN CALIFORNIA, ARIZONA, &c.

STEAMERS ON

NORTHERN COAST ROUTE

LEAVE SEMI-WEEKLY FOR FOLLOWING PORTS:

POINT ARENAS,   PORT TOWNSEND,
   MENDOCINO CITY,   SEATTLE,
      EUREKA, CAL.,   TACOMA,
         HUMBOLDT,   VICTORIA,
            PORTLAND, OREGON,   BRITISH COLUMBIA,
AND ALL POINTS IN OREGON AND WASHINGTON TERRITORY.

The Steamers of this line are FIRST-CLASS IN EVERY RESPECT, sail punctually, and passengers can rely on courteous treatment.
   This is the cheapest and most comfortable route to above-named points. No disagreeable staging over dusty roads, magnificent views of the Golden Gate and Coast Scenery.

☞ *Tickets purchased via this line include meals and room on Steamer.* ☜

Freight Consigned to this Company will be PROMPTLY FORWARDED and CHARGES COLLECTED ON DELIVERY

N. B.–Mark goods care G. N. P. S. S. Co., San Francisco.

GOODALL, PERKINS & CO.,   D. B. JACKSON,
   AGENTS, SAN FRANCISCO, CAL.   *Gen'l Pass'r and Ticket Agent,*
                                          No. 214 Montgomery St., San Francisco, Cal.

This timely advertisement announces the beginnings of the Pacific Coast Steamship Company. Courtesy Stanford University Library

day were being shipped in this fashion, and by the end of 1874 over 6,000 tons of grain had been thus transported, with the railroad averaging over $600.00 per day in revenues. In this short period of time joint rail-ship freight rates to San Francisco had been adjusted to about two dollars per ton less than that of the rival Southern Pacific. In addition, passenger service was quite substantial, with the roundtrip fare of $1.50 per person being charged.

By 1875 traffic had increased so much on the M&SV that the need for a second locomotive was generated. Shortly thereafter, a brand new 4-4-0 slimline Baldwin arrived on the property to carry the number 2 and the name *Monterey*. Soon it was hard at work pulling M&SV passenger trains at the maximum exhilarating speed of eighteen miles per hour and the slower freights at twelve miles per hour over the line.

Because of David Jacks's large investment in the M&SV, and because he was one of its officers, it soon became his practice to give out free passes to various influential friends for different religious and civic purposes. Several of the other officers were also contributing to this free patronage. Eventually, it got so bad that more people were riding for free than were paying. To correct this, President Abbott convinced the board of directors to pass a resolution that henceforth and forevermore only officers and employees of the company could ride for free. A short time later the Reverend McGowan of the Episcopal church, one of the more respected religious leaders of the community, approached President Abbott about a pass. Both Abbott and Jacks wanted to extend such a courtesy to Mr. McGowan, but the new resolution forbade it. To solve the problem and at the same time meet the requirements of the railroad, Abbott had McGowan declared the railroad's official chaplain, and the pass was issued. As a result, the M&SV became the first railroad in California, and possibly the United States, to have its own chaplain.

Abbott's tricky railroad maneuvers extended beyond religious favors into the political arena. On one occasion a Democratic rally was to be held in Monterey. The Monterey Central Committee inquired as to the lowest rate for an excur-

Monterey & Salinas Valley Railroad.

TIME TABLE

TO TAKE EFFECT AUGUST 4, 1876, AT 8.00 A. M.

For the Government and Information of Employes Only.

Trains leave Monterey at	8.00 A. M.	Trains leave Salinas City at	3.15 P. M.
Arrive at Bardin's at	8.50 "	Arrive at Castroville Crossing at	3.30 "
" Castroville Crossing at	9.15 "	" Bardin's at	3.55 "
" Salinas City at	9.30 "	" Monterey at	4.45 "

FLAG AND OTHER SIGNALS.

1. A red Flag by day or a red Light by night, displayed on the front of an engine, shows that another train is following, which has the same rights as the engine or train bearing the signal.

2. A white Flag by day or a white Light by night shows that an extra engine or train will pass over the road in the direction in which the Flag or light is carried, but will keep entirely out of the way of all regular trains. Work Trains and Track Parties must be kept entirely out of their way and give a clear track to them. Engineers and Conductors of Trains bearing a white Flag or white Light, will be particular and call the attention of **Meeting Trains, Station Agents** and all others concerned, and explain the meaning of it.

3. **One sound of the Whistle** is the signal to apply the brake.

Two sounds of the Whistle is the signal to let go the brakes.

Three sounds of the Whistle is the signal to back the train.

Four sounds of the Whistle is the signal to call in the flagmen, and when approaching a station to have a man attend the switch.

4. **Several short sounds of the Whistle** is the signal of danger; and when on the road a signal of that kind is given, and the train comes to a stop or is standing still, section men in hearing distance will go to the assistance of the train, as it then becomes a signal of distress.

5. **Night Signals.**—A light swung over the head is a signal to go ahead; when swung across or at right angles with the track, is a signal to back up, and when moved up and down is a signal to stop.

6. **Any Violent Signal** or Demonstration given with a Light at night or with a Flag, hat, cap, or with the hands by day, must be considered a signal of danger, and the train brought to a stop until its meaning is understood.

A. GONZALEZ, Superintendent.

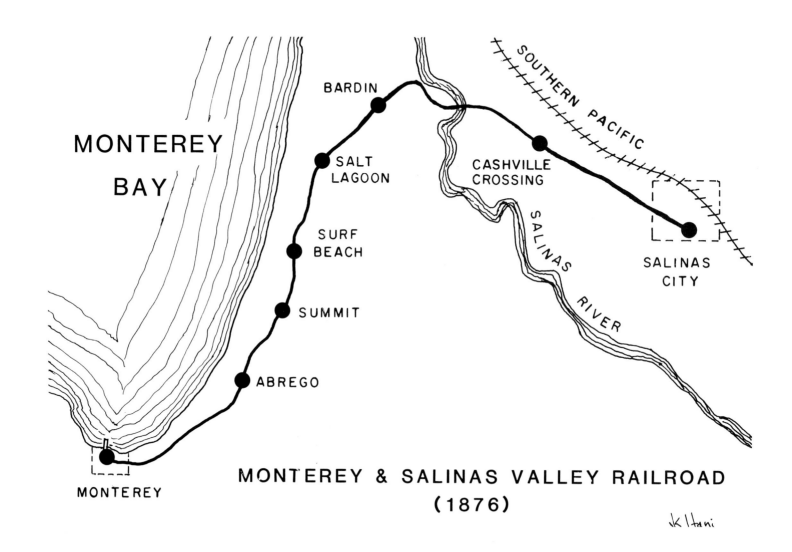

MONTEREY BAY

BARDIN

SALT LAGOON

CASHVILLE CROSSING

SOUTHERN PACIFIC

SALINAS RIVER

SALINAS CITY

SURF BEACH

SUMMIT

ABREGO

MONTEREY

MONTEREY & SALINAS VALLEY RAILROAD
(1876)

The Monterey & Salinas Valley Railroad yards as they appeared at Monterey in 1875. Photograph courtesy Fred C. Stoes Collection

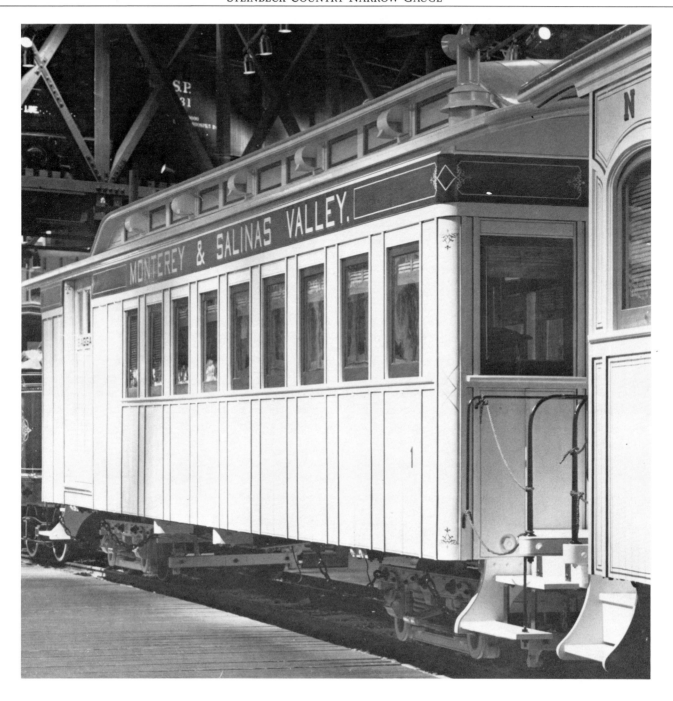

sion from Salinas to Monterey to attend the rally, and Mr. Abbott quoted a figure. Mr. Abbott then turned right around and contacted the Republican Central Committee in San Francisco and asked them to send their very best speaker to Salinas to talk on the same night. On the day of the simultaneous events he had signs posted in Monterey announcing a free excursion to Salinas. That night there was a very good turnout from Monterey attending the Salinas Republican meeting, while the Democratic rally had very few people in attendance from Salinas. Later, Mr. Abbott admitted it was a dirty political trick, but also that anything was proper in political matters.

As the new year of 1876 approached and the old year of 1875 came to a close, the affairs of the railroad were reviewed with much satisfaction. The Monterey & Salinas Valley had turned a handsome profit in its first year of operation and, even though there had been a cost overrun of $150,000 during construction, the future based on current earnings looked bright.

Unfortunately, the M&SV was on a collision course with time, the elements, and some very powerful people. The winter of 1876–1877 was the driest year ever in the recorded history of California; less than five inches of rain fell in the Salinas and Pajaro valleys. As a result, the railroad's freight business proved disastrous. The following year the weather reversed itself and was extremely wet, producing a tremendous yield in grain. Just about the time the railroad expected to see itself recover because of a bumper crop, an unseasonal June rain destroyed most of the standing grain in the fields. This included 6,000 planted acres belonging to President Abbott that failed to yield a single sack of grain. Mr. Abbott pledged his credit to keep the line in operation, but the loss of his crops and the subsequent demands of his creditors, which caused him to lose his heavily mortgaged 16,000-acre San Lorenzo Rancho, ruined him financially. Soon a call went out for a $10.00 per share assessment to keep the line solvent.

Perhaps the first narrow gauge passenger car to be manufactured and delivered in California, this completely restored M&SV Carter Brothers piece of work resides for all to see in the State Railway Museum at Sacramento. Photograph by Bruce MacGregor

It met with little success, as most of the other farmers were in a similar financial position and unable to help the railroad.

Seeing the opportunity before it, the Southern Pacific made an unsuccessful attempt to purchase control of the M&SV by picking up the delinquent stock. Next, they lowered their shipping rates to below that of the Monterey & Salinas Valley. As a result, the narrow gauge began to lose patronage to the Southern Pacific and fell deeper and deeper into debt. Finally, operations were suspended.

In August of 1879 the Southern Pacific purchased the Monterey & Salinas Valley Railroad at a foreclosure sale. Shortly thereafter, a new standard gauge line was constructed from Castroville to the Monterey & Salinas Valley at Marina. The line from Marina to Monterey was standard gauged and later extended to Pacific Grove and Lake Majella. The portion of the narrow gauge from Salinas to Marina was abandoned.

Shortly after the foreclosure sale, Charles Crocker of the Southern Pacific sold the entire Monterey & Salinas Valley Railroad, including locomotives, rolling stock, nineteen miles of track, turntables, and water tanks, to the Nevada Central Railway. For the next fifty-eight years the same equipment that had operated as the M&SV would live out its usefulness hundreds of miles from its original home.

As for President Abbott, he moved on to a new and sobering life in Arizona. David Jacks, on the other hand, while losing thousands of dollars in the bankruptcy of the line, stayed to become a multimillionaire.

The Prophecy

While the Southern Pacific dominated the California Central Coast freight and passenger traffic during the 1870s, there were a couple of other successful entities in the 1880s and one more in the 1890s that definitely put a kink in the SP's local profits.

In 1876 the Pacific Coast Steamship Company had been established on the western shores of California by Charles Goodall and George Perkins to go after the lucrative coastal

The Monterey & Salinas Valley Railroad has been replaced. This standard gauge Southern Pacific train, comprised of a high-wheeled, American-type locomotive and passenger-carrying caboose, poses with its crew at Monterey, ready to take on duties that were only a short time ago handled by the narrow gauge. Photograph courtesy Guy Dunscomb Collection

Before there were railroads up and down the West Coast, the only quality transportation to places like Los Angeles, Seattle, San Diego, Portland, and San Francisco was by ship. One such ship was the Pacific Coast Steamship Company's State of California, *shown above. All during the 1880s and 1890s this 2,266-ton coastal iron lady made many intermediate stops at Santa Cruz and Monterey, serving Steinbeck Country with elegance and distinction. Photograph courtesy University of California, Santa Cruz Special Collections*

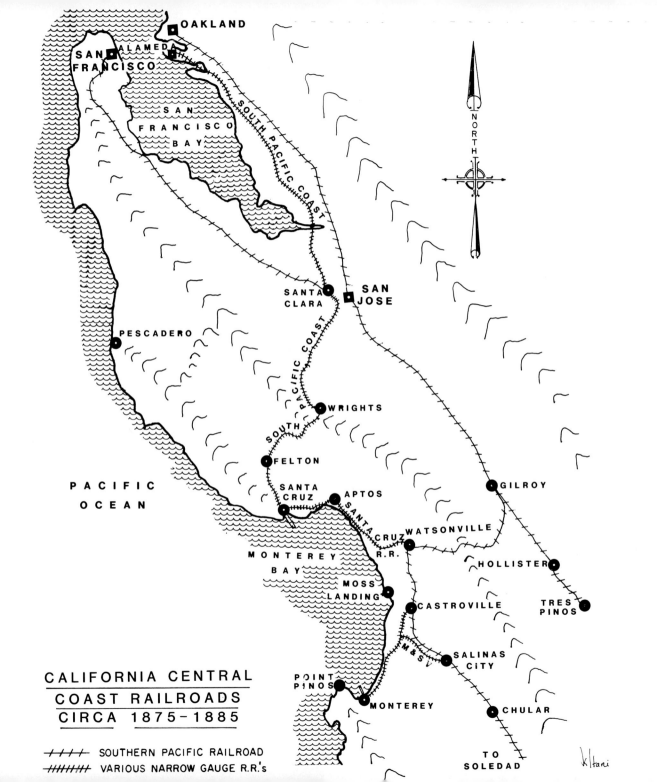

OAKLAND

SAN FRANCISCO   ALAMEDA

SAN
FRANCISCO
BAY

SOUTH PACIFIC COAST

NORTH

PESCADERO

SANTA
CLARA   SAN
JOSE

PACIFIC COAST

WRIGHTS

SOUTH

FELTON

PACIFIC
OCEAN

SANTA
CRUZ   APTOS

GILROY

SANTA
CRUZ
R.R.   WATSONVILLE

MONTEREY
BAY

HOLLISTER

MOSS
LANDING

CASTROVILLE

TRES
PINOS

M & S

SALINAS
CITY

POINT
PINOS

CALIFORNIA CENTRAL

MONTEREY

CHULAR

COAST RAILROADS

CIRCA 1875-1885

TO
SOLEDAD

Kitani

/+/+/ SOUTHERN PACIFIC RAILROAD
/#/#/#/# VARIOUS NARROW GAUGE R.R.'s

traffic. In setting up their many ports and connections along the coast, they had purchased Captain Moss's operations at Moss Landing together with Hudson's Landing on Elkhorn Slough and much additional property from David Jacks for $16,000. In doing this, they had re-established the port of Moss Landing with a full-time agent, S.N. Laughlin, to look after any and all business for their normally scheduled ship, the *Vaquero.*

They soon started picking up quite a bit of business from the Southern Pacific by charging only $3.75 per freight ton to San Francisco instead of the $4.75 per ton charged by the SP. Because they had a goodly amount of capital behind them, and because they were a large seagoing operation, the Southern Pacific could not successfully bully them or buy them out. Thus, the Pacific Coast Steamship Company became thorn number one in the side of what was otherwise a monopoly held by the SP.

Thorn number two came in the form of one Nevada Comstock millionaire, Senator James Fair. Fair in 1880 successfully completed a top quality narrow gauge railroad, the South Pacific Coast, from San Francisco, via ferry to Alameda, down the East Bay to San Jose, and over the Santa Cruz Mountains to the company's long wharf at Santa Cruz. The South Pacific Coast thus cornered the early 1880s lumber market in the Santa Cruz Mountains and it offered lumbermen, merchants, and farmers in Santa Cruz and Santa Clara counties an alternative to San Francisco, along with direct connections to Pacific Coast Steamship Company ships at the Santa Cruz wharf.

From the foregoing it is easy to see why Elliot & Moore's *History of Monterey County, 1881* made the following prediction with regard to the area's transportation future:

> It has been said in reference to Moss Landing, that it could, at less than a tithe of the cost of Wilmington Harbor, be turned into a dock harbor. It will probably be the terminus of a narrow gauge railroad running up the valley to compete with the Southern Pacific. . . . the extension of the South Pacific Coast Railroad cannot be long delayed. The era of railroad building in this valley has in truth only commenced.

Although Steinbeck Country history would later record the name of the prophecied narrow gauge railroad as the Pajaro Valley Consolidated, Elliot & Moore's glimpse into the future was correct. The Pajaro Valley Consolidated Railroad, lasting almost forty years, in conjunction with the Pacific Coast Steamship Company, would prove to be one of California's most successful independently owned narrow gauge operations and of prime importance to the growth and development of Steinbeck Country.

In later years the Del Monte Hotel, would become the SP show-place along the Monterey branch, with famed trains like the Del Monte Limited making daily round trips from San Francisco to its very door. Photograph by Jean Andrus

II / SUGAR AND THE PAJARO VALLEY

Claus Spreckels and the Sugar Industry

MUCH HAS BEEN WRITTEN OF CLAUS SPRECKELS and the vast industrial empire he created during his lifetime. A German immigrant, he arrived in the United States in the late 1840s with the equivalent of seventy-five cents in his pocket. His first job was that of a grocery clerk, but before long he owned the store in which he worked. Thus began his heralded rise in the financial and business world.

By the end of 1862, Spreckels had bought and sold grocery stores in Charleston and New York City and a grocery store and brewery in San Francisco. At the young age of thirty-five he was already quite wealthy, but this was only the beginning of his business ventures and industrial empire. Unlike many others who had been caught up in the local glitter of gold, he was not interested in the then-flourishing mining industry. Instead, his first large-scale financial venture was into an as yet untried and untapped market.

While in the grocery business, Spreckels had observed that there was a large and relatively unfulfilled demand for sugar on the West Coast. This, coupled with the fact there were no western refineries, meant that a very high price was being paid for a very precious commodity. Spreckels soon concluded that if he were the one to open a western sugar refinery, he might be able to mine his own form of granulated gold.

In 1863 he organized a group of investors and formed the Bay Sugar Refinery in San Francisco to go after this white gold. Soon he was importing raw cane sugar for the company from the Sandwich Islands (Hawaiian Islands) and re-fining it into finished West Coast product. He also began to personally acquire large sugar plantations in Hawaii, and in 1867 he formed his own San Francisco company, the California Sugar Refining Company. Now in full control, he began to pursue his own destiny.

"Sugar King" Claus Spreckels. Photograph courtesy Amstar, Spreckels Collection

As the West Coast population continued to expand, the demand for sugar in San Francisco significantly increased. Eventually the city's refineries became strained beyond capacity. In 1881 Spreckels, seeing profits at hand, built a $1,000,000 cane sugar refinery. According to experts, it was the most modern such facility in the United States.

Before long Spreckels began to eliminate competition on the West Coast by either purchase, merger, or price wars. He gained control not only of Hawaiian sugar production, but also of the political, financial, and shipping concerns of the islands. And while he professed to deplore monopolies, Spreckels at one time controlled the production and distribution of cane sugar in the area that stretched from Hawaii to the Mississippi River. It is reported that during this period Spreckels paid twenty-five percent of all taxes in Hawaii. With his technologically new methods and cheap labor, he could produce sugar at a lower cost than it could be produced anywhere else. Eventually, he came to be known as the "California Sugar King."

In addition to the production of sugar, Spreckels was also involved in steamship lines, real estate, railroads, and public utilities. While some of these activities were related to sugar, others were the result of his ability to recognize a worthy investment or his inclination to accept a challenge.

Western Beet Sugar Company

In 1872, Claus Spreckels, while looking for a place he could really call home, purchased 2,390 acres of a Spanish land grant in Aptos, California, near Soquel. Before long he had made it a showplace with an elaborate home, a hotel, guest cottages, and a race track and polo field for his thoroughbred horses. While he had a beautiful Nob Hill mansion in San Francisco, he and his wife preferred to spend as much time as possible at their Aptos estate. Spreckels through the ensuing years became well acquainted with the area and its local business leaders, even to the extent of becoming involved in the Santa Cruz Railroad. He built a wharf here and loaded local lumber on ships bound for his holdings in Hawaii.

In time he also became aware of the potential of the Pajaro Valley for growing quality sugar beets. Previous attempts to produce sugar on a large scale from California-grown beets had met with limited success, not for lack of good raw material, but for lack of business acumen. Since his power and influence in Hawaii had begun to diminish, Spreckels decided to get completely out of the cane sugar business and to concentrate his energies on the production of beet sugar. Perhaps he could succeed where others had failed.

In the fall of 1887, Claus Spreckels put his beet sugar plans in motion by inviting two prominent Watsonville men, Mr. W.R. Radcliff and Mr. W.V. Gaffey, to his home in Aptos to discuss the possibility of building a sugar factory in their town. Spreckels had just returned from Germany, where he had purchased factory machinery and a year's supply of seed, and he was looking for a place to use them. No doubt enjoying the moment, he teased Radcliff and Gaffey by stating that he expected to build a beet sugar factory somewhere in California, and he named a number of towns that had offered to donate land. He also readily let it be known that he preferred Watsonville as the site, but that the land for the factory would have to be donated to induce him to locate there. After listening to Spreckels, both men were convinced that the factory would be a great asset to the area and were willing to give it their full support. They couldn't wait to spread the word.

It didn't take long for a followup meeting to take place between the local Watsonville and Pajaro Valley farmers and business leaders and Claus Spreckels so he could formally present his proposal. After seeing the facts and figures, the farmers were thoroughly convinced they could make more money growing sugar beets than the current crop of grain. To add incentive, Spreckels offered to contract for 2,937 acres of beets, with an additional premium added for the five-, ten-, and twenty-acre parcels producing the largest amount of sugar per acre. As a final incentive, Spreckels offered to give technical help in the art of growing the beets.

After the meeting, the November 10, 1887 Watsonville *Pajaronian* carried the following quote to support Spreckels's intentions:

I am now in my sixtieth year and it would kill me to fail in what I undertake to do. It is not money that is an object to me, but I want the people of California to be able to show that Claus Spreckels has done something for this state when his bones are at rest.

On December 7, 1887, Spreckels accepted a gift deed to a twenty-five-acre factory site located west of Walker Street, in Watsonville. Local citizens contributed $13,140 to buy the site. Most of the money was raised in Watsonville, with the largest sum coming from Charles Ford of the Ford and Sanborn Company. Money was also contributed from Santa Cruz—lumberman and long-time business associate, Fred Hihn, led the support with a $600 contribution.

Spreckels, being a man of action, soon put the wheels of progress in motion. On January 19, 1888, the Western Beet Sugar Company, as it was to be known, under the careful guidance of its newly handpicked chief engineer and general manager, William C. Waters, began construction on what would become the largest beet sugar factory of its time in the United States. The main building itself, which would house all the German-built processing machinery by Maschinenfabrik & Grevenbroich, would be six stories tall and would measure over 280 feet in length and 65 feet in width when completed. Adjoining the main building would be the boiler house, where ten steam engines of 400 horsepower each would be located to provide the mill's power. External to these main buildings would be the 900-foot-long beet receiving and storage bins. To allow all this construction to take place, which included the use of over 1,600 barrels of cement, and to later provide for the delivery of beets and the shipping out of beet pulp and raw sugar by rail, a spur track was laid from the Southern Pacific Watsonville Depot to the site.

In almost no time at all the gala day of April 18, 1888 was at hand. Attorney Julius Lee had been chosen orator for the day's events. Since early morning local townspeople and other citizens from the surrounding Pajaro Valley had been gathering in Watsonville. Now they and other visiting dignitaries, such as E.B. Pond, mayor of San Francisco, were lining the depot platform to greet the arriving train that carried Mr. and Mrs. Spreckels and their guests. The town band had also been assembled and was busily playing rousing tunes of the day to the seeming delight of all gathered.

At last, the big, high-wheeled Southern Pacific American type locomotive with the Spreckels party in tow rounded the curve and slowly came to a stop. Mr. and Mrs. Spreckels and their invited entourage disembarked from the train, and the festivities revolving around the laying of the Western Beet Sugar Company Watsonville factory cornerstone had begun. First, a lavish reception was held at the Mansion House Hotel. From here, the procession moved to the factory site for the dedication by Attorney Lee. And so the cornerstone was laid in place that day amid fanfare and applause and speeches and bouquets of flowers. More importantly, and fully realized by most in attendance, Watsonville had received a financial plum which meant prosperity for many and the establishment of a local agricultural industry which exists in a somewhat more modern form to this day.

The first "campaign," as a sugar production season is known, was in 1889. The line of farm wagons on opening day, loaded with the first yield of locally grown sugar beets, extended about eight blocks from the factory to downtown Watsonville. Unloading the wagons was a very slow process, as it was done by hand. It wouldn't be until some years later that steam donkey engines would be used to expedite the procedure. Farmers were paid $4.00 per ton for beets delivered to the factory, and during this first campaign 15,000 tons of sugar beets were processed.

The rich alluvial soil of the Pajaro Valley produced beets that contained the highest percentage of sugar ever recorded in the world. This included those grown in Germany, which until then had been the leader in beet sugar technology and production. On an average, 350 tons of beets produced 45 tons of raw sugar.

While the new Watsonville factory was an almost immediate success, there was one disappointment: due to the rapid expansion and increased tonnage, only raw sugar could be produced. This meant that once the raw sugar was produced, it had to be sent to San Francisco via the Southern Pacific for refining in a Spreckels cane sugar refinery. It was against Spreckels's business principles to be dependent upon the Southern Pacific for the delivery of beets and the shipment of the raw sugar. The Southern Pacific was gaining thousands of tons of new business due to his Watsonville factory, and it was his thinking that their rates were higher than necessary, and that there was no guarantee they wouldn't raise them still higher.

Spreckels had often spoken out against monopolies, but he himself had gained control of the cane sugar industry by eliminating the competition. When he was dissatisfied with the shipping companies to Hawaii, he bought ships and started his own line. When he was insulted by an official of a San Francisco utility company, he built his own power company and they later paid dearly to buy him out. To Spreckels, a monopoly existed when the competition was eliminated and then the rates or costs were raised to produce much more than a fair return on an investment. Spreckels's success was basically due to his sound business management and ability. He believed he had eliminated much of the competition fairly, and though he controlled the western sugar industry, it was his belief that his sugar prices were reasonable to the public.

Once again Spreckels put some facts and figures together and came to the conclusion that by building a narrow gauge railroad from the factory to the wharf at Moss Landing, he could take advantage of the cheaper steamship rates to San Francisco. It also occurred to him that once this line was established he could extend it a little farther into the farmlands of the Moro Cojo and tap thousands of additional acres of the potentially rich beet growing areas of the lower Salinas Valley.

Even with his own railroad, Spreckels realized he would still be highly dependent upon the Southern Pacific for a large percentage of his sugar beet shipping. Yet he also realized that his railroad would give him a significant amount of working leverage for dealing with the SP in the future.

The Pajaro Valley Railroad

Formal articles of incorporation for the Pajaro Valley Railroad were filed with the county clerks' offices in Monterey and Santa Cruz counties and the California secretary of state's office in Sacramento during the month of January 1890. The road was to be a steam-powered three-foot narrow gauge, twenty-four miles in length, running from the city of Watsonville to the city of Salinas. The company's capital stock was listed at $1,000,000 and was comprised of 10,000 shares at a face value of $100.00 each. The directors and officers of the company were John D. Spreckels, president; James B. Stetson, M. Ehrman, John L. Koster, M.L. Jones, and Leon Sloss – all of San Francisco. All stock had previously been subscribed to and was held either by the directors or the Spreckels family. William C. Waters, in addition to his duties at the Western Beet Sugar Company factory in Watsonville, was chosen to be the road's superintendent and general manager. The main corporate offices were housed in the Spreckels Building in downtown San Francisco.

Thus, the die had been cast, on paper anyway. Before the opening of the next beet campaign it looked as though the Pajaro Valley Railroad would be a reality and Claus Spreckels would once again hold the transportation trump card.

One of the first orders of business for the new railroad was the surveying of its intended roadbed. To accomplish this the company hired a local surveyor from Santa Cruz, and later the county surveyor for many years, the well-qualified Mr. Thomas Wright. In short order Mr. Wright was at work establishing footings, taking bearings, locating bridge sites, determining elevations, and evaluating various curvatures with

Although this picture was taken in February of 1983, the lock itself dates back to the original Pajaro Valley Railroad. Photograph by Rick Hamman

regard to train length and rail wear. Of initial importance was the 9.8 mile section between the Western Beet Sugar Company factory and the wharf at Moss Landing and then the short 2.6 mile extension to a site on the Moro Cojo Ranch. This was to be the first leg of the railroad constructed so that the 1890 beet season could be adequately handled. As soon as this portion was completed and in operation, construction would begin on the rest of the line from Moro Cojo to Salinas.

The proposed right-of-way, as surveyed by Mr. Wright, was to be essentially level; the high point was twenty feet at Watsonville, and the low point was five feet at Moss Landing. While there were to be no tunnels, as the line would skirt anything that approached such an elevation, a number of rather substantial trestles were required. This was because the road would be constructed mostly through the lower Monterey Bay tidelands and sloughs and near the mouths of, and along, the Pajaro and Salinas rivers.

For the most part, there was no problem in securing the necessary deeds to the rights-of-way. The farmers were more than anxious to have such immediate access to a railroad that offered them both sea and land connections. Prices for parcels of land ranged from a low of $1.00 to a high of $1375.00. The exception to this was the Watsonville Fruit Packing Company, which saw the railroad coming and charged almost $4,000.00 for a small piece of property that just happened to be needed for the freight warehouse and depot. Fortunately for the railroad, the Watsonville yard and engine house were to be located on the factory grounds, which were already owned by the company.

Shortly after the incorporation of the Pajaro Valley Railroad and during the time of the survey the following notice appeared in several West Coast newspapers:

NOTICE TO CONTRACTORS

Sealed bids will be received by the undersigned up to April 30th, 1890, for the construction of 12 miles of Standard Narrow Gauge railroad for the Pajaro Valley Rail Road Co. in Santa Cruz and Monterey Counties, Cal.

1st. For the complete construction of said road including culverts, cattle guards, cuts, fills, pilings, placing of ties, laying of rails and putting road-bed into a surfaced condition complete for train service.

2nd. For the grading of road-bed and placing of culverts, cattle-guards and ready for ties.

3rd. For piling, capping, placing stringers and ties ready for rails.

4th. For laying ties and rails, placing road-bed into surfaced condition complete for train service.

Maps, profiles, specifications and other information may be had on Thursdays, Fridays and Saturdays at the office of the Western Beet Sugar Co., Watsonville, Cal. where the road begins.

Ties, rails, fish-plates, fish-plate bolts and rail spikes will be furnished by the Pajaro Valley Rail Road Co. to contractors alongside of said road at Moss Landing, Monterey Co., Cal.

The right is reserved to reject any or all bids.

W.C. Waters, Supt.
P.V.R.R. Co.
Watsonville,
Santa Cruz Co.
Cal.

The construction contract was awarded to J.B. McMahon & Son, 22 Howard Street, San Francisco. The railroad agreed to furnish the contractor with equipment and labor at the following rates:

Item	Cost/Day
Locomotives: (including Engineer, Fireman, Conductor, and coal)	$25.00
Flatcars:	1.00
Dumpcars:	.50
Horses or mules: (including feed)	1.00
Teamsters: (including board and room)	40.00/month
Use of Cookhouse: (including wood and water)	3.00
Blacksmith/helper: (including use of Blacksmith shop – no material included)	5.00
Boilermaker, Machinist, and Carpenters: (including helper)	5.00

The contractor will be responsible for any damage to the above equipment.

Pajaro Valley No. 1 as it appeared before leaving the Baldwin Factory. Photograph courtesy Broadbelt Collection

By the middle of May 1890, J.B. McMahon & Son had the construction of the Pajaro Valley Railroad well under way. Initially, until a portion of the new road was opened for construction trains, all materials arrived via the Southern Pacific at Watsonville and Pajaro (Watsonville Junction) and by steamship at Moss Landing. The gravel ballast and most of the right-of-way fill for the roadbed came from a quarry at the Pajaro River Bluffs, 5.4 miles from Watsonville. Much of the mainline rail, thirty pound, was purchased used. All new rail, forty-five pound, along with spikes and fishplates, was purchased from Pacific Rolling Mills in San Francisco. In addition, a total of 93,000 pounds of miscellaneous car parts and equipment was purchased and received from the SF&NP Railway Co. of Northern California.

The only construction projects not undertaken by the contractor were the grade crossings of the Southern Pacific Santa Cruz Branch at Watsonville and the Monterey Branch at the Moro Cojo Ranch just west of Castroville, and the laying of a third rail on the Southern Pacific factory spur so that narrow gauge locomotives could be used to switch standard gauge cars within the grounds. During the summer of 1890, the Southern Pacific agreed to install the crossings at a cost of approximately $1,400.00 each and to sell the factory spur, install a parallel spur of 1,445 feet, and to allow a third rail to be laid on both spurs, with the SP spur third rail extending as far as the Watsonville Depot. The additional spur was included to handle the large amount of sugar beets being delivered by the Southern Pacific, along with the limestone used in the manufacturing process and the wood and coal used to fire the factory and locomotive boilers.

One would imagine, based on the Southern Pacific's sphere of influence during these "Octopus" days and its previous bloody encounter with Claus Spreckels during his building of the competing San Francisco and San Joaquin Railroad (later part of the Santa Fe) down the San Joaquin Valley, that business dealings between the two roads would be less than cordial. This was far from the case, however; the Big Four realized that the Watsonville factory was a success, and the future freight revenue to be gained from the operation would more than off-set any losses to the narrow gauge and the steamship companies with which it connected at Moss Landing.

To meet the construction and initial operating needs of the railroad, two twelve-ton 2-4-2 Saddle Tank locomotives were ordered through the Williams, Dimond & Co. offices in San Francisco, agents for the Baldwin Locomotive Works. These two locomotives, labeled P.V.R.R. No.1 and No.2, were delivered to the Western Beet Sugar Company factory via the Southern Pacific in time for construction use. In addition to the necessary motive power, an initial order was placed with Carter Brothers for six ten-ton boxcars and six ten-ton flatcars, two cabooses, and an undisclosed number of finished two-and-a-half-ton beet dump cars. In addition to this, a short time later two more flatcars were ordered along with extra parts to make enough beet dump cars to fill out the roster to 100 working units. These were shipped via steamer from Alameda to Moss Landing, and all had arrived by August of 1890.

To make the harvesting and transportation of sugar beets from the fields to the new Pajaro Valley Railroad work more smoothly, the company purchased portable track on which to run the horse- and mule-drawn beet dump cars. The track, purchased from Minnigrode & Co. of New York for $3,700.00, was comprised of a mile of straight sections, twenty sixty-foot-radius curved sections, and three right-hand and three left-hand switches. To make the use of the track as flexible as possible, the twenty-pound rail and metal ties were shipped predrilled but unassembled, so they could be riveted together as needed.

At last, the summer of 1890 had come, another beet campaign was in progress, and the Pajaro Valley Railroad had been completed from the Western Beet Sugar Company factory in Watsonville to the Pacific Coast Steamship Co. wharf at Moss Landing. The railroad was unofficially operating beet trains that far. By the first week in September the line had been finished the 12.4 mile distance to the Moro Cojo Ranch, and commercial operations had begun.

While there is no record of a gala celebration to honor the

It's sugar beet loading time on the Moro Cojo Ranch, and Mr. Gaffey, sitting second car back, has the situation well under control. Photograph courtesy Pajaro Valley Historical Association

opening of the railroad, there must have been a day during that summer when Claus Spreckels, family members, and invited guests reviewed his little line. Let's try to recapture what the day and the time and the life of those present must have been like.

All during the previous night and well into the early morning hours, the seemingly silent and motionless summer fog had nestled low over the fertile Pajaro and Salinas valleys, surrounded by the Santa Cruz and Gabilan mountains. Now it was grudgingly giving way, with ever increasing frequency, to small blue vaults of warm sunlight. The recently furrowed ground and its attending atmosphere lay in quiet presence, ready for the coming of some special event. The Pajaro and Salinas rivers meandered cautiously, seeming to gingerly pick their way to the gently rolling Monterey Bay, so as not to disturb the awakening day. But a feeling of commencement, of expectation, of excitement was pervading this tranquil scene. The day had come. Soon, Claus Spreckels would be seeing the fruit of still one more financial endeavor in his long list of accomplishments.

The newly constructed three-stall, seventy- by forty-eight-foot Watsonville roundhouse stood fixed in time, its wooden walls gently resonating in calm harmony to some soft panting from within. A short sigh was heard, and then a number of almost inaudible bursts of energy filled the air. Suddenly, the pert little PVRR locomotive No.1, with steam up, quietly emerged and rolled to a rhythmical stop at the foot of the turntable. Engineer Wyckoff and Fireman Porter climbed down from the cab and moved the fifty-foot truss into place. Next, the engine was carefully guided onto the span, swung around 180 degrees, and run out to the factory siding where the day's activities were to begin.

Already waiting at the siding were Claus Spreckels and family, Superintendent Waters, other officials and guests, Conductor Huff and Brakeman Hanson, along with the morning local's consist of four boxcars loaded with raw sugar bound for Moss Landing, a flatcar with makeshift benches surrounded by guardrails, and a new caboose. Slowly, the little Baldwin 2-4-2 backed up to the morning train, the link and pin couplers were set, and the Pajaro Valley Railroad mixed train No.2 was ready for departure. Two blasts on the whistle, the release of brakes, and this narrow gauge, sugar-hauling dignitary express was under way.

Out of the Watsonville Yards and onto the main went this jaunty little special at the breakneck speed of fifteen miles per hour, following the route of the newly laid iron due south for about a mile across the rich farmlands of the lower Pajaro Valley. It was warm and clear by now, but the moisture left from the early morning fog pinked the cheeks of those passengers daring to ride exposed on the flatcars. Soon, at the Pajaro River, the train drew ohs and ahs from those on board as it began to make the 1,904-foot, sixty-degree curved trestle crossing. At this time of the year the river was a mere trickle, but during the rainy season it was known to fill its banks and sometimes go beyond, as the railroad would painfully find out several times in the future.

Once on the other side, the train turned west along the Pajaro's southern bank and more or less followed the river's course through the fertile valley for the next five miles to its mouth on Monterey Bay. As the train came closer and closer to the outlet, the temperature began to drop, and those on the flatcar were no longer sure it was the best choice of vantage point. They soon were renewed in spirit, however, as they had their first beautiful glimpse of fine-grained sand and pounding Pacific Ocean surf. In later years this area would come to be known as Sunset Beach, and would be viewed and visited by thousands of pleasure-seeking beachgoers.

Near the mouth of the river the train once again turned southward along the land side of the sand dunes parallel to Monterey Bay. After about another mile and a half of gentle rattle and clank, this mixed No.2 special came to a gradual stop at a point near the beach. Here, everybody disembarked and walked out onto the soft sand to get their own firsthand view of peaceful, half-moon shaped Monterey Bay. Later in the road's life, when passenger service was instituted, this place officially

Schooners load and off-load the product of the day at the PCSS Co. wharf, Moss Landing. Photograph courtesy Pajaro Valley Historical Association

became the well-known stop of "Beach."

It was 11:00 A.M. by the time everyone had stopped lingering on the beach and had returned to the train. By now it was shirt sleeve weather, and everybody was looking forward to the rest of the day's activities with much more anticipation and curiosity. In short order, Engineer Wyckoff was at the whistle cord signaling "off brakes," and brakeman Hanson was then seen jumping from boxcar to boxcar releasing the brake wheels, which had been set at five percent to keep the train from rolling. Gradually the little drivers on the PVRR No.1 began to rotate and to gather momentum as this dinky engine and its train moved on down the line a short distance to the mouth of the Salinas River. Once there, this sauntering mass of locomotion and attached tonnage drifted around a slight curve to the southeast, along the eastern bank of the river. Then it continued on to the Elkhorn and Moro Cojo sloughs and its first official business of the day at Moss Landing.

Just before reaching the Elkhorn Slough, at the place where it met the Salinas River, the train slowed to a crawl so Claus Spreckels and all on board could get a better look at the approaching trestle and entrance to the Pacific Coast Steamship Company wharf on the Island. First, the train had to traverse a 608-foot trestle paralleling the county road crossing over the Elkhorn Slough. Then, after a short curve to the southwest, it had to make a second crossing of 528 feet over the Moro Cojo Slough to reach the intermediate destination of Moss Landing. For the train to then get to the wharf, a wye had been installed. Its western leg crossed the Salinas River on a third 406-foot trestle before gaining access to the Island. Ever so carefully the surefooted little Baldwin steed guided its following consist over the first two trestles and halted in the eastern tangent of the wye. Next, the train was broken in two between the flatcar and the boxcars, and the four loads of raw sugar were run out over the river and onto the Pacific Coast Steamship Company siding, later to be moved onto the wharf for unloading and transfer to one of its many coastal ships. Finally, the PVRR's other two empty boxcars were picked up to be taken to the end of track for use on the Moro Cojo Ranch. With

the train once again made up, this four-car special got under way to the satisfaction of all its passengers.

The final 2.6 mile portion of this 12.4 mile trip was rather uneventful – the right-of-way was more or less a very level and very straight line along the Salinas River into the heart of the Moro Cojo Ranch. Once at the end of the track, the two boxcars were cut out, and the two-car train, consisting of the flatcar and caboose, was made ready for its return trip to Watsonville. As for Claus Spreckels and family, company officials and invited guests, all spent the rest of the day wandering the rich farmlands of the local area and enjoying the refreshments brought along for this special occasion.

On the warm, starlit early evening trip home, the cares of all on board turned into a gentle rolling and swaying purr of relaxation, and all agreed that the day's activities had been a most splendid success.

Projects carried to completion seldom resemble the initial concept behind them. So it was, of course, with the Pajaro Valley Railroad. Initially, it was conceived to be an extension of the Western Beet Sugar Company into the fields where the beets grew and also a less expensive way to get raw sugar to Spreckels' plant in San Francisco for final processing. It soon became apparent, however, that with a shipping connection to the Pacific Coast Steamship Company at Moss Landing and the possibility for freight and passenger connections with the Southern Pacific at Watsonville, the Pajaro Valley Railroad was destined to be far more than originally planned.

As the winter of 1890–1891 came and went and plans were made to complete the right-of-way from the Moro Cojo Ranch to Salinas, it also became obvious that the railroad's business would be expanding and that additional equipment would be necessary. The two new Baldwin 2-4-2T locomotives had proved to be too light and not powerful enough to handle the expected increase in traffic. As a result, an order was placed in April of 1891 for a new, and much larger, 2-6-0 Mogul type Baldwin beauty to be PVRR No.3. This twenty-three-ton coal-burning slimline locomotive would more than take care of

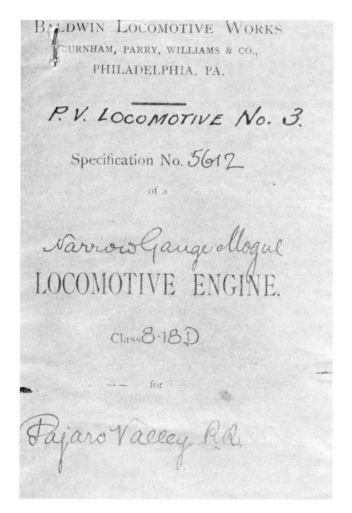

These two photographs are actual views of the covers of the original Baldwin specifications for the Pajaro Valley Railroad's first heavy power. Locomotive No. 3 was ordered in 1891, a year before locomotive No. 2 was ordered. Photographs courtesy Carl Gatske

the road's additional motive power requirements, or so they thought. Shortly after the engine was ordered, a second order was placed with Carter Brothers in San Francisco for fifteen more fifteen-ton flatcars, at a cost of $425.00 each. These cars were to be constructed of Oregon pine, have a length of twenty-eight feet, and be equipped with twenty-six-inch wheeled arch bar trucks; the same construction and design as those built for the nearby South Pacific Coast. When completed in the Carter Brothers Newark Shops, the flatcars would carry PVRR numbers 109 through 124.

In May of 1891, bids were let for the completion of the railroad from Moro Cojo to Salinas. The railroad was to again furnish all rail, ties, fishplates, and spikes, and the contractor was to construct the roadbed and lay all ties and rail such that the right-of-way would be ready for train service. Once again J.B. McMahon & Son of San Francisco was awarded the bid. The connection between the railroad and McMahon & Son is probably lost to history, but they were always the contractor to win the cut glass fly swatter when it came to major PVRR construction awards.

No real problems were encountered in completing the 23.6-mile narrow gauge line to Salinas (Tucker Station). The right-of-way had already been purchased during the previous construction, and the extension was essentially straight and flat. Therefore, the surveying by Charles L. Pioda, later to be PVRR general manager and superintendent, went very quickly, and grading and track laying soon followed. Within six months the line was completed and in operation at the unbelievable cost of only $4,735.00 per mile.

By the end of July the additional Carter Brothers flatcars had arrived at Moss Landing via a Pacific Coast Steamship Company ship, and shortly thereafter, on August 5th, locomotive No.3 with tender arrived via Southern Pacific flatcar at Watsonville. Now the railroad could get on with its anticipated second busy freight season and its second beet campaign, and none too soon, either. Already the company's busy little 2-4-2 tank locomotives and twelve mainline cars had been responsible for the movement of 315 carloads of freight during

the month of July, and that didn't include any sugar beets. In August the company books reported that the obviously overworked line carried 770 carloads of freight and 210 carloads of sugar beets. In September it carried another 125 carloads of various freight for the local farmers and ranchers and over 470 carloads of sugar beets.

A goodly amount of the non–sugar beet freight hauled by the Pajaro Valley Railroad, including a surprising amount which came across the platform at Watsonville from the Southern Pacific, was destined for Moss Landing and the Pacific Coast Steamship Company. An agreement had been worked out between Claus Spreckels and the PCSS Co.: 25 percent of all freight revenue jointly generated would go to the railroad and 75 percent would go to the steamship company. In support of this, the PCSS Co. had a regular schedule that required ships such as the *Gipsy,* the *Alex Duncan,* the *Navarro,* the *Record,* and the *Yaquina* to make scheduled stops at Moss Landing on Wednesday and Saturday of each week. In this fashion the PCSS Co. served the PVRR and other narrow gauge operations, including some of its own, all up and down the West Coast. In time this service came to be known as the Narrow Gauge Route.

By the conclusion of the 1891 beet campaign and freight-hauling season, it had become painfully obvious that the two little Baldwin tank engines and the one stalwart class 8-18D Mogul were woefully inadequate to meet the needs of the railroad. The tank engines were just too small for mainline long train operation, and that left the lone Mogul to do the work. As a result, the company decided to get rid of one of its small engines and replace it with another 2-6-0 Mogul. In March of 1892, according to company records, locomotive No.1 was probably sold to the E.L. White Lumber Company up the coast, locomotive No.2 became No.1, and an order was placed for a second Baldwin Mogul, class 8-20D, to become the second No.2. The word "probably" is used regarding the disposition of No.1, since there is some question to this day as to whether No.1 or No.2 was sold.

From 1892 through 1895 the day-to-day life of the railroad

Pajaro Valley No. 2 is about to move a heavy beet load off the Moro Cojo Ranch. Photograph courtesy The Society of California Pioneers

didn't change very much. During this time passenger service via caboose was started, as no passenger equipment had been purchased; minor right-of-way realignment and firming up, which had been left unfinished during construction, was taken care of; trestles that had been hastily put up to get the PVRR in operation were filled in; new rolling stock, consisting of ten fifteen-ton boxcars and twenty fifteen-ton gondolas, twenty-eight feet in length with three-foot hinged sides to facilitate the dumping of beets, were ordered from the J.S. Hammond Car Company; and the right-of-way, which ran along the southern bank of the Pajaro River, was substantially reworked due to persistent flooding during the rainy season.

During this period, the long Pajaro River trestle crossing near Watsonville also saw major reconstruction. At the time the original 1,904-foot structure was constructed, the present-day system of levees and dams did not exist to control the heavy winter runoff. As a result, there was always the danger of debris building up at the trestle, especially in the main river channel, threatening adjacent farmlands and the railroad itself with flooding. To resolve this problem, the railroad replaced the trestle sections over the main channel of the river with a single 128-foot span, and accomplished major rework of 1,048 feet of trestle during May of 1893. As usual, the work was done by McMahon & Son, who were able to do the entire job without disturbing the day-to-day operation of the PVRR. When completed, the remodeled structure, built on a sixty-degree curve, could handle two sixty-ton locomotives with train at a one-ton-per-square-foot loading, with the trains moving at a maximum speed of thirty miles per hour.

By 1896, Claus Spreckels's Pajaro Valley Railroad was a well-established entity in the local farming community, hauling grains, potatoes, apples, dairy products, and various other commodities. It had more than fulfilled his original intent for it to effectively meet the transportation needs of the Western Beet Sugar Company factory at Watsonville. Still, he was dissatisfied. First, the Southern Pacific was continuing to charge him exorbitant rates for what they were hauling. Second, the shipping of raw sugar to San Francisco for final processing, no matter how cheap, was an additional expense. And third, the Watsonville factory, even as modern as it was, still couldn't handle all the sugar beets that could be grown in the local area. Perhaps Claus Spreckels concluded, "I'll have to think about this and see if I can come up with a better solution."

Watsonville, California. Sugar beets are delivered to the factory, apples are loaded aboard SP refrigerator cars, and the late afternoon passenger train from San Francisco has just arrived. Photograph courtesy Charles Ford Co.

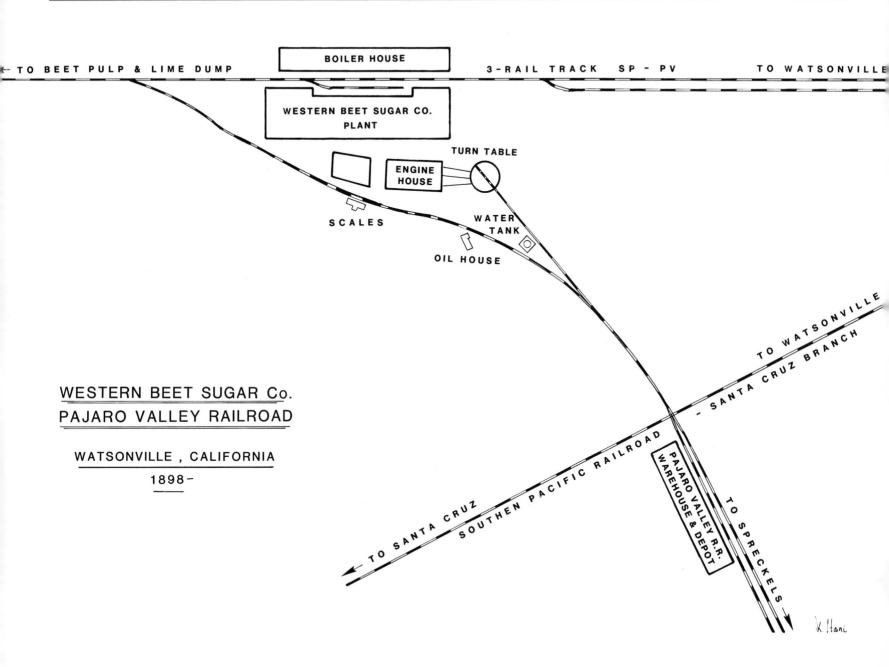

TO BEET PULP & LIME DUMP

BOILER HOUSE

3-RAIL TRACK   SP - PV   TO WATSONVILLE

WESTERN BEET SUGAR CO. PLANT

TURN TABLE

ENGINE HOUSE

SCALES

WATER TANK

OIL HOUSE

TO WATSONVILLE

SANTA CRUZ BRANCH

WESTERN BEET SUGAR Co.
PAJARO VALLEY RAILROAD

WATSONVILLE , CALIFORNIA
1898-

TO SANTA CRUZ

SOUTHEN PACIFIC RAILROAD

PAJARO VALLEY R.R.
WAREHOUSE & DEPOT

TO SPRECKELS

K. Hani

The Pajaro Valley Railroad depot and freight warehouse at Watsonville sees a busy afternoon. Photograph courtesy Pajaro Valley Historical Association

A PV engine runs light along the beet dump track. Photograph courtesy Pajaro Valley Historical Association

Pajaro Valley No. 3, the engine house, the turntable, and the Western Beet Sugar Factory all pose for this classic picture. Photograph courtesy Pajaro Valley Historical Association

The Western Beet Sugar Company/Pajaro Valley Railroad/Watsonville beet dump. Photograph courtesy Pajaro Valley Historical Association

In addition to being an obvious source of quality sugar, the beet and its processing also had some excellent side benefits. Among other things, the used lime carbonate proved to be a fine fertilizer, and the beet pulp a prime cattle feed. Shown here is the three-rail track leading to the lime and beet pulp dump. Initially the pulp was dumped into a tapered pit 20 feet wide at the bottom and 75 feet wide at the top. Overall the pit was 30 feet deep and 600 feet long and was capable of holding over half a season's beet pulp residue. Pulp was removed from the factory to the pit by an aerial tramway with buckets. During the campaign, thousands of head of cattle were brought onto the land near the pit for feeding. An overhead storage area was also constructed so that SP cars, and later narrow gauge cars, could be loaded with pulp for shipment. One of the largest buyers of the pulp was Spreckels's fellow countryman, Henry Miller, of the famed Miller and Lux Company. The pulp was shipped via the Southern Pacific to Miller Station, which was located at the headquarters ranch south of Gilroy. Photograph courtesy Pajaro Valley Historical Association

III / A LONG FUTURE FOR SOME, A SHORT PAST FOR OTHERS

THE WATSONVILLE FACTORY of the Western Beet Sugar Company, in a short six-year period, had become even more successful than Claus Spreckels envisioned it would be. The introduction of sugar beet cultivation to the local Pajaro and Salinas Valley farming communities had been so successful that it soon spread to nearby San Benito, Santa Clara, and greater Monterey counties. In no time at all the Watsonville factory was at capacity, and the tri-county area potential for increased production could have filled several more factories of the same size. Spreckels, of course, wanted to capitalize on this situation; however, he had three stumbling blocks that would have to be hurdled before he could do so. First, the factory was beyond existing capacity, and its Watsonville site was not adequate for new construction. Second, the capacity of the San Francisco factory for final processing was likewise confined. And third, the supply of beets from the immediate area served by the Pajaro Valley Railroad, while more than adequate for the Watsonville factory, was not sufficient to support a new facility. Thus, to realize a profit from the expanding sugar beet production in the nearby counties, more and more of the tonnage would have to be hauled by the Southern Pacific, over greater distances, to an as-yet unspecified factory or factories.

Spreckels first plan to reduce shipping costs and at the same time accommodate the increased sugar beet supply was to build a series of limited capacity plants in the individual beet-growing areas. He discarded this idea, however, since past experience indicated that a series of smaller refineries, spread out over a wide area, would be hard to manage and control. Also, any savings in shipping costs would be lost to wasteful duplication of effort at the various locations. Instead, on July 18, 1896, Spreckels announced a new proposal, which called for the construction of a single larger plant at one central location, using the latest in new equipment, design, and technology. As before, a number of local California cities expressed an interest in having the factory in their community; however, the town of Salinas seemed to have best captured Spreckels's attention.

A hardy construction gang poses for the camera in 1897 on the factory site. Photograph courtesy Amstar, Spreckels Collection

On August 6, 1896, Spreckels called a meeting with local farmers and businessmen to discuss the growing of sugar beets and what would be necessary to build such a large factory in Salinas. First, James Bardin, a prominent local man, presented detailed facts and costs on sugar beet cultivation, which included planting, harvesting, labor (Chinese), and gross receipts as compared to the current crops of barley and grain. Next, Claus Spreckels outlined the factory requirements, which included a large growing area, an adequate water supply, a good transportation system, a sufficient work force, and a suitable building site.

The people of Salinas knew there was plenty of water available; they also knew that between the Southern Pacific, the Pajaro Valley Railroad, and the Pacific Coast Steamship Company transportation wouldn't be a problem; labor could be imported, so that left the building site in question. As an inducement for Spreckels to grace their town with his proposed venture, they offered him a few acres of land, free and clear, for the factory site, as their counterparts had previously done in Watsonville. This, to their surprise, did not sway him. Unfortunately, they didn't know that the factory he had in mind would require over 100 acres of ground. As a result, the meeting came to an end with Spreckels remaining uncommitted for the time being.

As time went on and local anticipation increased to a fervor, it became obvious to the people of Salinas that old Claus was still keeping them very much in mind. Every day many men would be seen out in the local area doing research and investigation into the depth of the water table and the quality of water available, the quality and substrate makeup of the soil, the price and availability of some very large parcels of land, and the extension of the Pajaro Valley Railroad from Tucker Station south for an undisclosed number of miles. Spreckels even went so far as to hire a tug and crew to take depth soundings off the mouths of both the Salinas and Pajaro rivers.

Because Salinas had a rural atmosphere and was a relatively small community, it didn't take long for the interest in the location of the Spreckels factory to be on the minds of most residents. A classic example of this was the following encouragement, which appeared on one of the menus of a local hotel restaurant: "Sugar Factory Stew, Chicken Ala Spreckels, Breast of Mutton Refinery Style, Fricandeare of Veal with Sugar Beets and Mass Meeting Ice Cream."

A New Factory

September 3, 1896, proved to be a very auspicious day for the Salinas Valley when Claus Spreckels appeared in Salinas and finally announced the location of the factory site. As could be guessed from the previous goings and comings of Spreckels's men, it was to be four miles southwest of town on the eastern bank of the Salinas River at a place to be known as Spreckels.

Claus Spreckels was never known to be a wool gatherer; by the end of the month he had the entire project well coordinated and in process. To begin with, 122 acres were purchased south of Salinas along Hatton Road at the Salinas River for the factory site. In addition, the Sillacci limestone quarry in the Gabilan foothills east of Salinas was purchased to supply limestone to both the new Spreckels and the old Watsonville factories. Up until this time limestone had been purchased from the Cowell Limestone Company in Santa Cruz and then shipped via Southern Pacific to the Watsonville factory. To reduce these costs, Spreckels acquired the necessary rights-of-way and started construction of his own narrow gauge line from the plant to the quarry and to the Pajaro Valley Railroad at Tucker Station. As a final measure, a right-of-way for the Southern Pacific was procured from their mainline near Salinas out to the factory site at Spreckels so that sugar beets could be brought in from all over to feed the ravenous appetite of this mammoth facility. If all went well, construction of the factory would start in January of 1897, and the first campaign at the new refinery would begin with the 1899 season.

It didn't take long, once the work got under way, for the local people to realize what a monstrous undertaking the Spreckels factory and supporting buildings was going to be.

The following account of the projected buildings, which appeared in an early 1897 edition of the Salinas *Californian*, describes such immenseness:

> The main office building, to be located along what is to be Spreckels Blvd., will be 75′ × 110′ and two stories high, built of brick, granite and slate, at a cost of $25,000.
>
> The factory buildings are to cover one hundred twenty-two acres, with 12,000 tons of concrete required for the foundations. The main factory building of brick and steel will be 106′ × 586′ and five stories high. Adjoining the main building will be a brick and steel boilerhouse 559′ × 68′ × 22′ high. The 12 boilers and four economizers will cost $140,000, with the boilers exhausting into two steel stacks 216′ high by 13′ in diameter and weighing 1,000 tons each. A power plant will furnish the factory with electricity.
>
> The brick and steel machine shop is to be 559′ × 40′ × 20′ high. In addition, there is to be a warehouse 20′ × 200′, an oil house 20′ × 32′ and a scale house 20′ × 32′, all of brick construction. In all 7,000,000 bricks are expected to be used. The quadruple mill, four sets of diffusions, will have a capacity of 3,000 tons of beets per day and produce 450 tons of sugar daily. For transportation, 5,400 feet of narrow and dual guage track will be layed on the factory grounds using 56 pound rail.
>
> Daily fresh water requirements are to be 13,000,000 gallons while fuel oil requirements will be 1,200 barrels or the equivalent in either wood or coal.

In February of 1897, Superintendent Waters went east for five weeks to inspect various pieces of machinery and the boilers under construction for the factory. As usual, Claus Spreckels felt the German processing equipment was far superior to anything the United States had to offer, so all such machinery would be coming from Germany. It was anticipated that the bulk of this United States and German equipment would be arriving at the factory site by August of 1897, so construction on the main and supporting buildings soon began in earnest.

The Risdon Iron Works of San Francisco had been awarded the contract for the fabrication and installation of all structural steel. This meant that thirty ironworkers and riveters would see steady employment for over a year. In all, before they were through on the factory site, they would build thousands of tons of structures, comprising over 200 standard gauge carloads of steel.

From the summer of 1897 to the summer of 1899 construction of the refinery continued at a steady rate. The large number of ironworkers, brick masons, and other craftsmen meant a boom to Salinas, as it had to supply housing and entertainment for them.

By August of 1899, the Spreckels factory was completed and ready to start both experimental and shakedown runs. The first beet delivery to the refinery was a five-ton wagonload from farmer Grimes, and the first run of beets through the factory was on August 24, 1899.

To better understand the scope of the project once it was in full operation and what it meant financially to the local farmers and business people and to Claus Spreckels, the following portion of an article he wrote in 1898 on the Beet Sugar Industry is presented:

> Last season's operations at Watsonville show an average of $56.24 per acre, gross returns, on the whole crop of over 150,000 tons. The average tons raised to the acre were slightly in excess of fourteen, and the price paid $4 per ton. The sugar produced amounted to nearly 20,000 tons.
>
> When the factory at Salinas is completed next year, we will be able to utilize the product of 30,000 acres. This area under beet cultivation will entail an expense of $22 per acre for labor and seed, aggregating $660,000. Sown in grain, the outlay would be under $160,000. The factory will have a capacity for crushing 3,000 tons of beets and turning out 500 tons of sugar daily. This is equivalent to a production of 60,000 tons of sugar for the working season of five months. When in full operation the daily disbursements will amount to $12,000 for beets, and $5,000 for labor and operating expenses—a total outlay for the season of fully $2,000,000. . . .

Below will be found a statement of the cost of raising, and profits derived from a beet farm located near San Juan (Bautista), California.

Item	Total Cost	Cost per acre	Cost per ton
EXPENSES			
Rent of 238 acres at $7.00 per acre .	$ 1,666.00	$ 7.00	$ .37
First plowing $340.00			
Second plowing 396.65	1,236.65	5.19	.28
Cultivating and harrowing 500.00			
Sowing-labor 85.00			
Use of drill 28.80	113.80	.49	.03
Seed, 2830 pounds at ten cents . . .	283.00	1.19	.06
Thinning, 1100 days at $1.00	1,100.00	4.62	.25
Cultivating and weed cutting, one man and two horses, thirty days at $3.00	90.00	.38	.02
Plowing out, one man and team, ninety-five days at $3.00	285.00	1.19	.06
Topping and loading into wagons, 1335.3 days at $1.00	1,335.30	5.61	.30
Hauling three miles to switch, at fifty cents per ton	2,225.50	9.35	.50
Freight on railroad to factory	2,225.50	9.35	.50
Cost of knives and hoes	20.00	.09	
Interest	300.00	1.26	.07
Total expenses	$10,880.75	$45.72	$2.44
INCOME			
4,451.275 tons of beets, at $4.00 .	$17,817.22	$74.86	$4.00
Sale of beet tops	200.00	.84	.04
Total income	$18,017.22	$75.70	$4.04
Net profit	$ 7,136.47	$29.98	$1.60

The main building and the boiler house is going up. Photograph courtesy California State Library Collection

Fortunately, local photographer Butler captured this view of the main building while under construction so that we today can visualize Spreckels's dream. Photograph courtesy California State Library Collection

The Spreckels Sugar Company factory is completed and in full operation. Photograph courtesy Amstar, Spreckels Collection

The latest in sugar processing and refining equipment has been installed in the factory and it is now ready for use. Photographs courtesy Amstar, Spreckels Collection

A house is moved by tractor to Spreckels to quickly provide accommodations for married men. Photograph courtesy Miss Rose Rhyner, Spreckels Sugar Co. Collection

A New Town

In 1897, commuting to work by private automobile was still in the future. Instead, it was the custom of the time for any company that did not build a factory adjacent to a town to provide its employees with adequate housing and the necessary commodities and amenities of life. So it was, of course, with the Spreckels Sugar Company and the new factory town appropriately named Spreckels.

Unlike most factory towns of the time, which were owned and operated by the company, Claus Spreckels had declared early on that his town would be the employees' town. First, it was to have its own separate utilities company. Likewise, all businesses would be owned and operated by entrepreneurs not connected with the sugar company. In addition, Spreckels further declared that none of the town's residents would be required to support the local business establishments as a condition of employment.

The town and the factory, while remaining separate entities to this day, started concurrent construction in 1897. The first building to be constructed in the new town was the sixty-room Spreckels Hotel, which was to house the majority of the single men working at the factory. Among other things, it boasted a kitchen and dining room complete with Chinese cooks and waitresses, a bar, a pool room, and a barber shop. To provide for the essential, staple, and social needs of the employees, a two-story building was erected on the southeast corner of Hatton Avenue and Spreckels Boulevard, which housed a general store on the ground floor and a dance and social hall on the second floor. The first proprietor of the store was the Ford and Sanborn Company (now the Charles Ford Company).

As the hotel did not provide for family living, and because Spreckels wanted the development of the town to get under way so his married men could be near the factory, a number of existing houses were moved to the Spreckels townsite to help supplement the new houses already under construction. Most of the new houses, along with the Spreckels Sugar Company

office building, were designed by architect William H. Weeks of Watsonville and later Palo Alto. Mr. Weeks was responsible for designing hundreds of houses and buildings of all types in the central coast area and later in the San Francisco Bay Area. Among his Spreckels designs was the plant superintendent's house, which was the largest in the community. It was followed by a smaller home with the exact same exterior appearance in another part of the community. Many of Mr. Weeks's homes were similar in design and construction.

In every developing family community a schoolhouse is a thing of civic pride and importance. In Spreckels, school was taught at first in the hotel, but as more families moved into the town, the school soon outgrew its quarters. Shortly before the turn of the century a two-room little red schoolhouse went up, and Spreckels students, under the careful tutelage of two dedicated teachers, improved their education.

Last, but not least, the railroad depot was constructed in 1899, and the thriving little town of Spreckels, California began to appear in major railroad timetables and schedules and in the Official Railway Guide. Obviously, it was a community of some stature.

For the town of Spreckels, the years from 1907 to 1918 were its most active and glorious period, and the two most important gauges of this activity were the hotel and the saloon.

Ever since its construction the hotel had been unable to provide sufficient housing during the factory season, particularly for bachelors. This brought about the construction of an annex in 1907, followed in rapid succession by five more annexes before the hotel stopped growing. Altogether, according to the August 23, 1907 edition of the Spreckels *Courier*, the seasonal population in residence at the hotel amounted to 1501 inhabitants. To satisfy the hunger pangs of these residents between meals, the hotel had a fifty-gallon coffee pot, a sixty-gallon stew pot, and a sixty-gallon soup pot going at all times. In addition to housing factory workers, the hotel also set rooms aside for regular service.

The saloon, known to the locals as the "Louve," was probably the only place in town besides the baseball diamond

Two formidable buildings, the Spreckels School House to the left and the company office buiding above, signal the obvious success taking place locally. Photographs courtesy Amstar, Spreckels Collection

that saw a larger congregation than the nondenominational church. It was here that on payday many of the single men would part with their hard-earned dollars for a little comfort and relaxation. It was also here that many of the married men would stop on a payday afternoon instead of going straight home. This practice upset some of the local wives so much that they once circulated a petition requesting that Spreckels be declared dry when all the liquor licenses expired in 1912. On another occasion, one of the largest scandals in the town's history transpired when the general store owner, Vollmer, began to sell cheap liquor at his mercantile and robbed the Louve of some of its clientele. Schroder and Steinfartz, owners of the Louve, countered by selling men's wear at a lower price. Soon after, Vollmer left town, selling out to Jess Juhler who renamed the store the Emporium. The store is still owned by the Juhler family.

Taken as a whole, the town of Spreckels resembled many other fledgling communities that were developing across the West. It had two newspapers, the Spreckels *Courier,* established in July of 1907 and existing until about 1915, and the Spreckels *Enterprise,* which saw publication from 1908 until 1918; it had a small jailhouse near the railroad depot looked after by a Monterey County assigned constable; it had a post office, originally located in the Spreckels office building and subsequently moved to its present location between the Emporium and the firehouse; and finally, it had the Spreckels Theater, or Opera House, opened in 1911 for the benefit of all.

As yet unmentioned, but of utmost importance, was the volunteer fire department. The Spreckels Volunteer Fire Department was organized in 1899 during a meeting held at the Pajaro Valley Consolidated Railroad depot. In the early 1900s the hose company, in addition to its normal volunteer duties, became quite a social organization. Among other things, it was active for many years in hose cart races at Salinas, Monterey, Hollister, Watsonville, Paso Robles, and other localities. Also, its annual picnic conducted at Alisal Park was said to be among the most enjoyable and sometimes the wildest of events. When the Louve closed, the fire department purchased it and converted it into the company firehouse. Later, when the new firehouse was built, the old firehouse was turned into a museum and local meeting hall.

Lastly, every burgeoning community has had its local town leaders and politicos. So it was, of course, with Spreckels. Its town fathers were known as the Board of Trade, and it was their job to look after the interests of the community. Typical of this activity was the following propaganda run in various newspapers up and down the state to attract business to the town.

> Under the Santa Lucia Mountains, lately named the Junipero Sierra, lies the town of Spreckels. It is a lovely spot on the Salinas River, seventeen miles from Monterey Bay. The Pajaro Valley Consolidated Railroad connects it with the steamers to the north at Moss Landing. Within sixty days a motor car will run every two hours to Salinas, five miles northwest of here. Sixty acres have been laid out for the enlargement of the town and for a public park.
>
> It enjoys a very mild climate and cool healthful breezes from the ocean in the summer. The town is thoroughly sewered and supplied with the purest of water. Spreckels has a school and the most skilled physicians and surgeons. It has a very large payroll the year round. No better place, or opportunity for building a new home or for entering business is offered anywhere.

Propaganda or not, the tactic proved successful, for soon Spreckels had allured businesses of all kinds: a meat market, a harness shop, a shoe and men's clothing store, a lumber yard, a livery stable, a cabinet shop, a painting and decorating service, a plumber, a bicycle shop, a laundry (Chinese), a barber shop, a saloon, a bank, a husband and wife doctor team, both physicians and surgeons, and last but not least, a grocery store operated by Wincey Yancey Wilson.

From that day to this the town of Spreckels has survived as an independent entity. Each year finds the city of Salinas encroaching closer and closer on its borders, but as of this writing there is still open space between the two communities. If you talk to the locals about Spreckels and its future, they seem to indicate that they like their little town the way it is and want to keep it unchanged. Only time will tell if they can succeed in doing so.

Spreckels became so prosperous during the Glory Years that it warranted a local bank. Photograph courtesy Amstar, Spreckels Collection

Inside the warm dining room of the hotel pictured above, the local ladies and gentlemen have gathered for a fine meal.
Right, the hotel is pictured during its prime. Photographs courtesy Amstar, Spreckels Collection

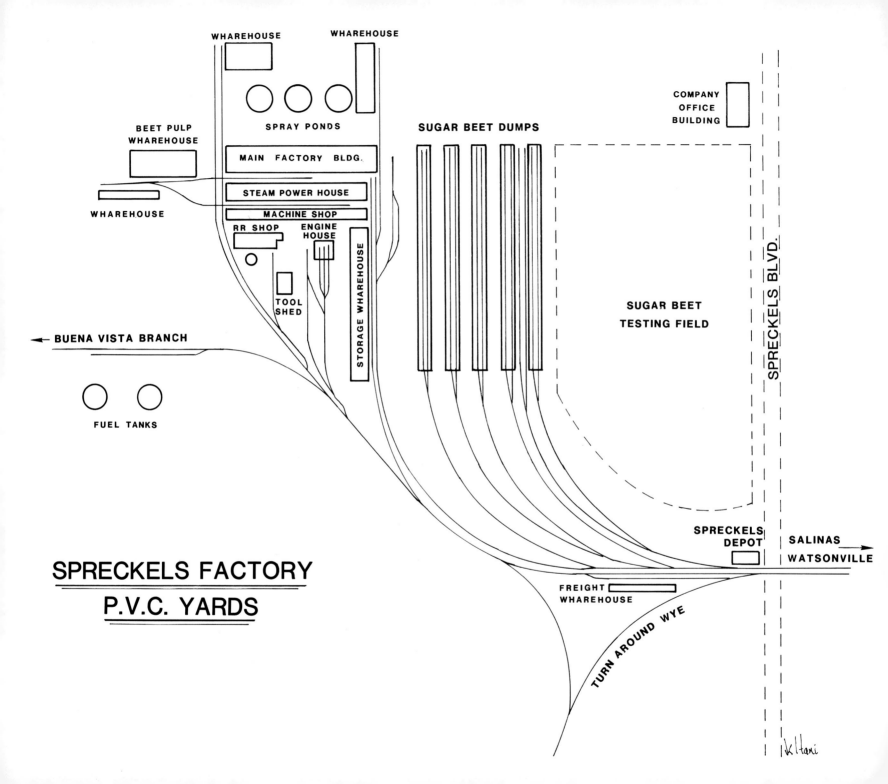

WHAREHOUSE

WHAREHOUSE

BEET PULP
WHAREHOUSE

SPRAY PONDS

WHAREHOUSE

MAIN FACTORY BLDG.

STEAM POWER HOUSE

MACHINE SHOP

RR SHOP

ENGINE
HOUSE

TOOL
SHED

STORAGE WHAREHOUSE

SUGAR BEET DUMPS

COMPANY
OFFICE
BUILDING

SPRECKELS BLVD.

SUGAR BEET
TESTING FIELD

BUENA VISTA BRANCH

FUEL TANKS

SPRECKELS FACTORY

P.V.C. YARDS

SPRECKELS
DEPOT

SALINAS
WATSONVILLE

FREIGHT
WHAREHOUSE

TURN AROUND WYE

It is wintertime in Steinbeck Country. The snow-covered Gabilan Mountains serve as a backdrop to the town of Spreckels while cumulus clouds gather threateningly overhead. Photograph courtesy Amstar, Spreckels Collection

Pajaro Valley No. 4 stands ready at the Baldwin factory to provide the railroad with much-needed new power. Photograph courtesy Broadbelt Collection

A New Railroad

On April 16, 1897, the narrow gauged Pajaro Valley Extension Railroad was officially incorporated to build the additional rights-of-way needed from the factory site to the Pajaro Valley Railroad at Tucker Station and the limestone quarry in the Gabilan foothills. First, a line was laid down 1.7 miles in length northeast from Spreckels (the factory site) to a point to be known as Watsonville Junction (not Pajaro). From here one branch of the road, the Alisal branch, continued in the same direction 5.1 miles farther to the quarry, while the other branch, considered the mainline, turned northwest for 1.9 miles to meet the existing Pajaro Valley narrow gauge. These extensions proved to be no real problem; within four months both lines were completed and in operation.

Basically, the Pajaro Valley Extension Railroad had been incorporated for the convenience of Spreckels & Company and their joint bookkeeping. It was a paper railroad with no rolling stock of its own and no employees. Thus, it came as no great surprise to anyone when, on December 9, 1897, the Pajaro Valley Consolidated Railroad was incorporated and the original Pajaro Valley Railroad and the Pajaro Valley Extension Railroad were absorbed by the new corporation. Interestingly enough, all the Pajaro Valley Consolidated Railroad stock was held by the newly created Spreckels Sugar Company, which itself was a combination of other Spreckels interests – the Watsonville Western Beet Sugar Company factory and the mammoth Spreckels factory soon to be completed.

Once again the down-home country narrow gauge out of Watsonville, which a lot of locals called the "Dinky Line," had taken on a larger stature. Soon this newly created Pajaro Valley Consolidated Railroad would be operating its pristine little trains over a 27.2-mile mainline and over an additional shortline branch, all for the benefit of the Watsonville and Spreckels refineries, the local residents, and the Pacific Coast Steamship Company at Moss Landing.

Almost immediately the PVCRR realized that it had nowhere near the necessary motive power and rolling stock to handle the increased business it was about to receive. Quickly, it set out to rectify this problem. First, three separate orders were placed for new engines with the Baldwin Locomotive Works via Williams, Dimond & Company of San Francisco. The new engines included another 2-6-0 Mogul, to be No.4 and lettered P.V.C.R.R., and two 2-6-2 tank engines, one labeled Western Beet Sugar Company, the other Spreckels Sugar Company. The Mogul was purchased to strengthen the PVC's mainline operations, while the tank engines were assigned switching duties at the respective Watsonville and Spreckels plants. For additional rolling stock to carry all the limestone from the quarry and the increased shipments of building materials and sugar beets, the Pajaro Valley Consolidated went back to the J.S. Hammond & Company car builders for seventy-five new gondolas.

By the time construction had begun on what was to become the largest sugar factory in the world, capable of turning out 350 tons of finished product per day, the little narrow gauge PVC was ready and capable of fully supporting it. On August 19, 1897, the steamer *Star of Russia* arrived at Moss Landing and began unloading some of the specialized beet processing machinery that had been purchased in Germany. In all, over 4,000 tons of machinery and materials were off-loaded at the Pacific Coast Steamship Company wharf for shipment to the new factory via the Pajaro Valley Railroad and later the Pajaro Valley Consolidated Railroad. Import duty on the machinery alone ran well over $200,000. In addition, the PVC also moved thousands of tons of gravel and sand from Quarry No. 1 about five miles north of Moss Landing to the factory site for its foundations and concrete work. When all was said and done, this spunky little slimline railroad had proven itself to be quite a respectable operation, generating almost $100,000 in yearly revenues by the turn of the century.

To meet the increased demand for raw product brought on by the production capability of the newly completed Spreckels Sugar Company factory, many previously dormant Pajaro Valley and Salinas Valley farming areas had been placed under the cultivation of the sugar beet. As a result, both the Pajaro

Spreckels Beet Sugar Co. No. 1, later PVC No. 9, pauses in front of the depot. Photograph courtesy Monterey County Historical Society

Pajaro Valley No. 4 heads for the water tank and turntable at Watsonville. Photograph courtesy Pajaro Valley Historical Association

Valley Consolidated Railroad and the Southern Pacific Railroad saw a tremendous increase in seasonal sugar beet traffic.

Although previous long-term plans made by the PVC were well intentioned, it soon became obvious, after only one season's campaign, that the railroad's capacity was still woefully inadequate. To once again try to solve this motive power and rolling stock shortage, the narrow gauge placed a new $22,000 order with Baldwin for three more mainline 2-6-0, class 8-20D Mogul locomotives, to be lettered P.V.C.R.R. and numbered 5, 6, and 7 respectively. In addition, it placed a second order with the J.S. Hammond & Company car builders for forty more gondolas and ten boxcars. The gondolas cost $400 each and were numbered 200 and 318 through 356, while the boxcars cost $575 each and were numbered 217 through 226.

Once all this new motive power and rolling stock had been delivered, the 1901 cumulative roster of the Spreckels Sugar Company owned PVC read as follows:

Locomotives	9	(two under other names)
Passenger Cars	3	(two Cabooses, one combine)
Gondolas	140	
Beet Cars	100	(four-wheel dump cars)
Boxcars	26	
Flatcars	15	

It is with this equipment roster that the Pajaro Valley Consolidated would enter its glory years of operation, when the train was the prime form of intercommunity transportation, and the auto, truck, and bus were of the future.

November 25, 1897. The Salinas Railway is looking forward to a long life on this their opening day. Photograph courtesy Monterey County Historical Society

The Salinas Railway

The Pajaro Valley Consolidated was not the only narrow gauge railroad in the area to come about because of entrepreneurial ambition. With over 700 men, many with families, living and working in Spreckels just four miles away, it didn't take long for the Salinas merchants and businessmen to realize that a financial bonanza of potential customers was theirs for the asking if only there was a way to get them to Salinas.

In short order the Salinas Railway was organized by a group of local citizens to provide transportation between Salinas, the Pajaro Valley Consolidated Railroad, and Spreckels. Formal articles of incorporation for the new railway were filed with the County of Monterey on June 12, 1897. On the board of directors were J.D. Carr, J.B. Iverson, W. Vanderhurst, P.H. Lang, John Berges, H. Winham, and Henry Bardin, all of Salinas.

The railway was capitalized at $100,000, with 4,000 shares valued at $25.00 each. The amount of stock subscribed to was only $26,925; an additional $1,500 was donated by the community, and another $15,000 had to be acquired through a first mortgage loan from the Monterey County Bank. The largest stockholder was the Vanderhurst-Sanborn Company with 190 shares. The largest single stockholder was J. McDougall with 60 shares. There was a total of eighty-nine stockholders.

The narrow gauge route surveyed between the two towns was entirely flat and involved no obstacles to easy grading and construction. Starting at the Southern Pacific Depot at Market Street in Salinas, the line went south down the center of Main Street to the edge of town, where the line shifted to the east side of Monterey Road (Main Street) until it got to Spreckels Boulevard. At that point, where the Monterey Road crossed the Salinas River, the line turned east and ran parallel to the south side of Spreckels Boulevard into the town of Spreckels. The line was surveyed a short distance beyond Spreckels, but no construction ever took place that far out. The railway was approximately five miles in length and cost $32,000 to construct.

For motive power and rolling stock the company purchased a new Vauclain compound 0-4-2 steam dummy from the Baldwin Locomotive Works for $6,500 and a used 2-4-2T Baldwin saddle tank engine along with three day coaches and a combination car from the Ferris & Cliff House Railroad for $7,840. This Ferris & Cliff House equipment had been in operation on California Street from Masonic Avenue to Land's End and Sutro Baths near the famous San Francisco Cliff House.

The railway began service by carting construction workers and laborers to the Spreckels Sugar Company building site. When the factory was finished, it brought employees. Although the little line provided excellent service between the two towns, it soon turned out that patronage was not sufficient to keep the line solvent. This was because most of the factory workers were single and lived not in Salinas, but in quarters provided by the company at Spreckels. Also, since the factory employed mostly seasonal help, the railway experienced extended periods of very low patronage. During the seasonal campaign the commuter employees who lived in Salinas did cause a heavy patronage period in the early morning and evening hours; however, this was not sufficient traffic to offset the rest of the year's losses.

In March of 1899, the Salinas Railway assessed each stockholder $3.00 per outstanding share to help bolster the company's sinking financial position. As if the railway did not already have enough troubles, the steam dummy locomotive broke down one morning on the trip to Spreckels. As the other locomotive was already down for repairs, the passengers were stranded until wagons arrived to carry them to their destinations. While the steam dummy was repaired and ready for service the next morning, the additional expense was an additional burden.

On February 18, 1900, a meeting was held with the stockholders in an attempt to stop the growing financial debt. To decrease losses, the number of trains operated were cut to two round trips per day. On March 5, 1900, the railway announced the following schedule:

Monday–Saturday:
Leave Salinas   6:25 A.M. and 3:00 P.M.
Leave Spreckels   9:00 A.M. and 6:00 P.M.

Sunday:
Leave Salinas   9:00 A.M. and 2:30 P.M.
Leave Spreckels   10:30 A.M. and 4:00 P.M.

In May of 1900, the board of directors, not wishing to assess the stockholders any further and unable to borrow any money, voted to shut down and abandon the line. The Salinas Railway, entirely dependent on passenger traffic, had failed after less than three years of operation. From the perspective of hindsight, perhaps the Salinas Railway was a premature venture based on the conditions at that time. If only it had been built just a few years later, its history might have been very different.

In August of 1900, a twenty-man crew tore up the rails and loaded them on Pajaro Valley Consolidated Railroad flatcars for shipment to Moss Landing, where they were loaded aboard a ship bound for a northern California logging line. The equipment was subsequently sold off under foreclosure to various buyers, including the San Jose & Santa Clara Electric, which purchased some of the cars and later converted them to trolleys to run on the Alum Rock Line.

Thus, the Salinas Railway became the second locally organized and owned railroad – the Monterey & Salinas Valley was the first – to go into bankruptcy. Once again the city of Salinas found itself mourning the loss of another homegrown idea that never reached its promised maturity.

The crew poses aboard Salinas Railway No. 1. Photograph courtesy University of California, Santa Cruz Special Collections

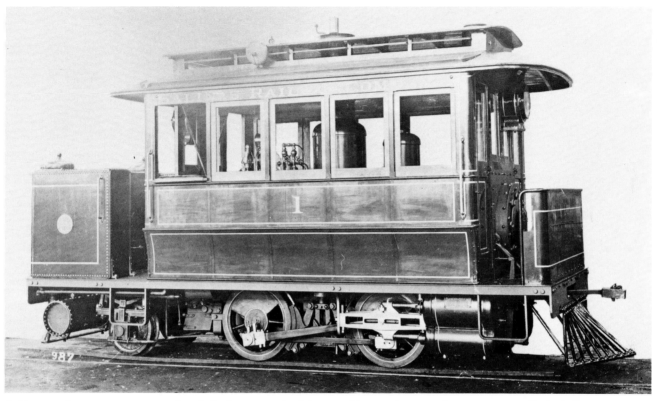

Salinas Railway No. 1 as seen shortly before its arrival from Baldwin. Photograph courtesy Broadbelt Collection

The End of the Beginning

Prior to the construction and operation of the factory at Spreckels, the Pajaro Valley Railroad sugar beet traffic had been from the south to the Western Beet Sugar Company factory at Watsonville. However, once the Spreckels refinery, with its much larger capacity, was in production, there was a reverse traffic flow from the north to the south. As a result, the only inbound Pajaro Valley Consolidated Railroad shipments to Watsonville were freight received at Moss Landing and farm products sent in for warehousing. As the beet traffic was seasonal, the railroad did everything in its power to attract additional inbound and outbound shipments of general freight and produce to Watsonville. But to no avail. With the exception of the passenger traffic, the northern portion of the Pajaro Valley Consolidated didn't see many trains.

It had been anticipated that once the new Spreckels factory opened the Watsonville plant would remain in operation to continue to meet the needs of the local farmers. This was not in the Spreckels Sugar Company plans, however, for as soon as the new refinery went into full operation, orders were given to shut down and dismantle the Watsonville factory. To somewhat pacify the disappointed Watsonville people, and at the same time make life easier for the local farmers, a new beet dump was constructed on the old factory grounds. This was necessary to facilitate the loading of sugar beets into PVC gondolas for the trip to Spreckels.

As a majority of the Watsonville factory grounds were no longer needed, sections of the property were offered for sale. As property was sold, trackage was either removed or relaid to meet the needs of the new owner. The main factory building and boiler house proved to be too large for use by any buyer, and they were eventually torn down. The main office building was moved to 318 Walker Street, where it remained for many years. Some of the machinery was sent to Spreckels, while most was sold for construction of a sugar factory in Fallon, Nevada. When this factory was later shut down, much of the machinery was repurchased and sent to Spreckels.

The railroad shops were moved to Spreckels, and since there was no longer any use for the three-stall roundhouse, it was torn down. Only the turntable remained. The railroad depot and warehouse were not on factory grounds and remained in limited use by the railroad.

And so went the Western Beet Sugar Company factory at Watsonville. What had originally been expected to have a long and prosperous future had died, leaving behind a very short past. When the score was finally tallied, all that was left was an empty Pajaro Valley Consolidated terminus and an infrequently used sugar beet dump, twenty-seven miles from a sugar factory that the people of Watsonville wished was still in Watsonville.

The Watsonville Transportation Company

The closing of the Western Beet Sugar Company factory at Watsonville had left many of the local citizens harboring considerable ill will toward Claus Spreckels and his enterprises. This was especially true considering the fact that the company had even gone so far as to sell off the land that had been given to them by the people of Watsonville only ten years before. This less-than-enthusiastic attitude spilled over onto the Pajaro Valley Consolidated Railroad and the connections it offered the Pajaro Valley farmers and ranchers to Moss Landing and beyond via the Pacific Coast Steamship Company. The Southern Pacific, whose freight rates weren't much better and whose concern for the local shipper and his problems was nonexistent, was likewise looked upon with much general disfavor. Thus, the prevailing feeling around town seemed to indicate that if there was some way for the locals to ship their product and produce and be provided with passenger service to San Francisco via transportation other than that belonging to the PVC or the SP, most would be ready to support such an operation.

Because of this psychological climate, it wasn't long before two San Jose business promoters, W.J. Rogers and H.H. Main, accompanied by three Watsonville men of means,

The Western Beet Sugar Company Watsonville factory sits idle. Soon, it will be no more. Photograph courtesy Pajaro Valley Historical Association

Robert W. Eaton, F.A. Kilburn, and Stephen Schurich, arrived on the scene and began preliminary planning and negotiations to give the people what they wanted. Their principle objective was to provide rail transportation from downtown Watsonville through the lower Pajaro Valley for approximately five miles to a wharf on Monterey Bay, where the company would then furnish water transportation to San Francisco. All this was to be done at a cost lower than the SP or PVC could offer and on a faster overall schedule.

All preliminary work came to an abrupt end on February 13, 1903, when the five gentlemen filed formal articles of incorporation for the Watsonville Transportation Company. Incorporators and officers of the company were: Eaton, president; Kilburn, vice president and treasurer; Main, secretary; Rogers, general manager; and Schurich, director. Capital stock was listed at $200,000 with 200,000 shares being subscribed to, most of which were locally owned.

The articles of incorporation described the intent of the Watsonville Transportation Company as follows:

> To construct a single or double track railroad of either narrow gauge or standard gauge, operated by steam engines, electrical power, gasoline motors or any lawful means of power, from the city of Watsonville along any feasible route to Monterey Bay at an estimated distance of five miles. Also to erect and maintain telephone and telegraph facilities and furnish electric current for such use as it may be put to use.

Also included in the articles was a declaration that the company proposed to operate a steam schooner from a port on Monterey Bay to San Francisco.

During the promotion of the railroad, various sites on Monterey Bay were considered for a port. It was agreed that the best port site was at Moss Landing, which had previously been selected by the PVC and the Pacific Coast Steamship Company. The coastline from Moss Landing to past Camp Goodall, north of the Pajaro River, was owned by the PCSS Co. This caused the best port sites to be eliminated, as the Watsonville Transportation Company wanted to be independent and free of any outside influence. Finally, a site north of the

PCSS Co. property was selected for the railroad's marine terminal. While the site was exposed to the open sea and not the best of geographical locations, enthusiasm for the railroad overcame any objections. The site was named Port Rogers in honor of the railroad's main promoter and general manager, W.J. Rogers.

The survey of the line was a snap, since the chosen route was essentially a straight and level line from Watsonville to Port Rogers. The line commenced on Wall Street at Main Street and ran out Wall to Beach Road, where it was constructed parallel to the south side of the road. At the beach the line curved north for about one-fourth of a mile around Camp Goodall and then turned west toward the Monterey Bay and on to the wharf under construction.

After much consternation, it was decided that the line would be narrow gauge and that its operation would be electric. Thus, as construction began two interurban-type cars were ordered, along with four flatcars and two boxcars. The electric cars served the dual purpose of carrying passengers and pulling the company freight cars. A powerhouse, freight warehouse, and car barn were built on Beach Road at or near the present site of Hiura Dryer. The electric line crossed the tracks of the Pajaro Valley Consolidated Railroad at this location, where an interchange was installed.

To complete the transportation service to be offered by the Watsonville Transportation Company via water connection to San Francisco, an order was placed for a new ship with the H.B. Bendixsen Ship Building Company of Eureka, California. This new ship, to be named the *F.A. Kilburn* after the company's vice president, was to be 175 feet in length with a 30-foot beam, and was designed to be one of the fastest steamships on the coast. Among other things, it was to have forty-five staterooms on the outer sides of the upper deck, and the hold below decks was to be devoted entirely to freight.

By May of 1903, the steam schooner *Aurelia* had arrived off the coast with most of the wharf piles and lumber and had unloaded same by high line to the beach. Construction of the wharf was well under way – over 400 feet of it were already

It's opening day for the Watsonville Transportation Company at Port Rogers. Photograph courtesy Pajaro Valley Historical Association

in place. The right-of-way and the placement of power poles was also well along with regard to grading and track laying; by early the following spring all would be in readiness to commence operations.

Like most grand openings, the Watsonville Transportation Company's opening on April 16, 1904 was no doubt considered a great success by those on hand. The day's festivities included ride after crowded ride aboard the electric cars and converted flatcars out to Port Rogers to greet the *F.A. Kilburn* as it arrived following its maiden voyage from San Francisco. In addition, once the ship docked with its seventy dignitaries and crew members, another short excursion to Santa Cruz and return was made, much to the delight of the Watsonville citizens who had never dreamed of such a possibility previously. By the end of the day all present agreed that a local opportunity had been seized, and that a bright future for the Watsonville Transportation Company was in the offing.

In no time at all the Watsonville Transportation Company operations were an accepted part of the daily comings and goings of the community. Each day would see car after car going from the park in downtown Watsonville out to the wharf and back with its avid beachgoers and tourists. Toward evening the freight and San Francisco-bound passengers would be transported out to Port Rogers and then loaded aboard the *Kilburn.* By early next morning the ship would have its freight and passengers in San Francisco, ready for the events of the day. After only eight such months of operation, the Watsonville Transportation Company had grossed a healthy $36,250 in freight revenues and another $13,750 in passenger fares.

While the railroad had been under construction WTC management had announced that the line would soon be extended four miles farther to the Vega district, and later to San Juan (Bautista), Hollister, and Gilroy. During July of 1904, surveys were carried out for such extensions. By September a $200,000 bond issue was voted on and approved by the company, and a contract was let to a San Francisco firm for initial construction of the line to Vega.

Mr. Main, secretary of the railroad, began making trips to Hollister and Gilroy to promote further expansion of the Watsonville line. He soon announced that with the proper inducements the line could be extended either to Gilroy and then on to Hollister or vice versa. This immediately created much rivalry between the two towns, as each wanted to be the first to have a coastal shipping connection at Watsonville, a fact of which Mr. Main was probably aware. As it turned out, Hollister was the first of the two to pledge patronage to the Watsonville Transportation Company. This, coupled with the fact that the railroad decided it would be cheaper to construct the Hollister extension, decided the question of which direction to go.

Within several months of beginning operations, however, the company suffered some unexpected financial setbacks that definitely slowed its expansion plans. Almost immediately after completion of the wharf at Port Rogers, Toredo worms began infesting the pilings. In a short time the end of the wharf had become so weakened that after the first fall storm 200 feet of it had to be replaced and major portions of the rest had to be repaired. Based on the theory that redwood, unlike pine, was not on the menu of the hungry little devourers, replacement piles were brought in from Green Valley. Just about the time repairs were being completed, heavy November storms and pounding waves struck, and the wharf was even more severely damaged. This time over 500 feet of pier had to be replaced. The cost of repairs due to both the worm and storm damage was put at $35,000. Fortunately, the company was able to survive the first year financially intact; however, the extension of the line to Vega, Hollister, and Gilroy had to be shelved, at least for the time being.

The company's solvency was to be very short lived. With the start of the heavy fruit and vegetable freight shipments, the Southern Pacific began to undercut the $3.00 per ton WTC rate between San Francisco and Watsonville. In no time at all the SP's freight rate was down to $1.50 per ton, and the Watsonville Transportation Company was left with its total revenues coming from the passenger business. To make matters worse, the *F.A. Kilburn* soon needed previously passed over

The F. A. Kilburn *is about to get under way for San Francisco from Port Rogers. Photograph courtesy Pajaro Valley Historical Association*

The Port Watsonville beach activities center. Photograph courtesy Pajaro Valley Historical Association

maintenance and had to be sent to San Francisco for repair. As a result, the only revenues being entered in the cash column of the company's books came from those few riders going between town and Port Rogers for recreation.

It was also during this financially depressed time that a dispute arose between some of the stockholders and the directors over promotional stock granted to Mr. Rogers and Mr. Main for services rendered. Some of the directors claimed they knew nothing of the transaction. The dispute reached such proportions that on August 12, 1905, the Santa Cruz County Grand Jury indicted Mr. Rogers and Mr. Main for misappropriating funds and falsifying records. The indictment was eventually set aside by the state appellate court on grounds of insufficient evidence. This court decision came much too late, however, to change the course of the events that were to immediately follow.

Influenced by the stigma of obvious improprieties, the Pajaro Valley Bank, on the same day as the grand jury indictment, attached the company for the $19,000 balance due on its first mortgage. This started a chain reaction among the other WTC creditors, and late that month the company went to court and started bankruptcy proceedings. On September 8, 1905, the Watsonville Transportation Company was declared bankrupt, and B.F. Brooks was named as trustee.

The *F.A. Kilburn,* which had been named the "Berry Boat," was taken over by Fred Linderman, a prominent San Francisco steam schooner operator and stockholder in the railroad. A short time later, while entering Coos Bay, Oregon, it lost its rudder, struck rocks, and tore a hole in its side. After being repaired at North Bend, Oregon, it continued in operation under various owners until June 14, 1918, when it caught fire and burned off the coast of Florida.

One would think that after receiver Edward White had been appointed to dispose of the Watsonville Transportation Company assets, it could have been accomplished in a reasonable amount of time. Unfortunately for both the stockholders and the citizens of Watsonville, the company's previous general manager, Rogers, kept the bankruptcy proceedings tied up in various California state courts for almost six years. In the interim, the wharf rotted, the right-of-way went to seed, and the floundering stockholders found themselves in a state of numb indifference until the spring of 1911, when the railroad was finally reorganized without the services of Mr. Rogers.

In this scene to the left, the Watsonville Transportation Company line is pictured headed west out of town on Wall Street. Above, the same view is seen again, this time from the opposite direction. Photographs courtesy Pajaro Valley Historical Association and California State Library, respectively.

Above, W.T.Co. car No. 2 is readied by its crew for the day's schedule, while right, car No. 4 is seen taking on passengers at the same location. Photographs courtesy University of California, Santa Cruz, Special Collections and Pajaro Valley Historical Association.

The Watsonville Railway & Navigation Company

On April 22, 1911, articles of incorporation were filed in the county court house at Santa Cruz incorporating the Watsonville Railway & Navigation Company. Its stated purpose was to "rehabilitate, construct, operate and maintain freight and passenger service between the City of Watsonville and the City of San Francisco by electric railway and steamers." Officers and directors of the company were F.E. Snowden, C.H. Fisher, C.A. Shuey, Golden W. Bell, and E.M. Heaney. Mr. Snowden of Berkeley was elected president. The company's capital stock was listed at $100,000 with a par value of $10.00 per share. In anticipation of a revitalized railroad and renewed service to the community, over $24,000 worth of stock had been locally subscribed to.

Right after incorporation, President Snowden announced that service to the beach would start the next week. The right-of-way, cars, powerhouse, and beach pavilion were being cleaned up and repaired. The track on Wall Street between Main Street and the Southern Pacific tracks on Walker Street would be abandoned. The railway rolling stock at this time consisted of one electric car, ten flatcars, and four boxcars. Previously, the WTC had had two electric cars, but one had been destroyed by a fire while in storage in 1909. The flatcars were equipped with benches and railings for passenger service.

A $60,000 contract to construct a new wharf was awarded to E.W. Hartman of the Marine Concrete Construction Company. The new wharf was to be 1,900 feet long and 20 feet wide except for 500 feet, which were to be 44 feet wide to support the freight warehouse and double track. To complete the project, 400,000 board feet of lumber and 500 concrete piles were to be required. For some unknown reason this contract was cancelled, and a new contract for a conventional timber pier 1,600 feet long, using the remains of the old wharf, was awarded to the San Francisco Bridge Company. Piles for the wharf were delivered by the steam schooner *Polson*.

The name of the port was changed to Port Watsonville. There appeared to be a genuine interest in revival of the port; several coastwise steamship companies, including the Pacific Coast Steamship Company, asked for docking privileges. The Pajaro Valley Development Company bought the beach land adjacent to the wharf and subdivided it into lots selling for $150 to $500. The California Pacific Company, a group headed by F.E. Snowden and his associates, acquired more beach land and promoted the tent city resort of Calpaco, a complex comprising sixty tent units complete with board sidewalks and running water.

The Port of Watsonville, its surrounding environs such as Camp Goodall, the wharf, and the beach would exist in a Camelot-like state for a short, but precious, three years. Each summer Sunday would find "Snowden's Giants" playing the baseball teams from surrounding towns on the port diamond. Afterward, a band concert would usually be held. As the day waned, the twenty- by fifty-foot dance pavilion, designed by W.H. Weeks, would become a popular gathering place. And at night, a moonlit ride aboard the electric line back to Watsonville was a favored way to cap the day's activities.

As it did in Camelot, however, tragedy brought an end to this idyll. In December of 1912, disaster struck one more time. Heavy storm-driven seas swept Monterey Bay, pounding and destroying 160 feet of the new wharf. After the seas had subsided and the weather calmed, a survey of the aftermath revealed $40,000 in irrepairable damage. This financially crippled the company.

In a last-ditch effort to save the floundering railway, Snowden filed suit against the San Francisco Bridge Company, constructors of the wharf, charging faulty construction and improper placement of piles. Snowden claimed the piles had been driven into the sand so hard that they were weakened and broken below the water line. The effort was to no avail however, as the suit was eventually dismissed by the court.

After this latest of disasters, Snowden was unable to find anyone interested in financing the railroad and its wharf any further. The railroad, unable to withstand the elements of Monterey Bay, shut down for good in October of 1913. In November the Union Trust Company of San Francisco, holders

The ballpark is groomed, the Watsonville Railway & Navigation Company right-of-way is in tip-top shape, and soon it will be a busy summer Sunday afternoon at Port Watsonville with the Snowden Giants in action. Photograph courtesy Pajaro Valley Historical Association

It has been a while since the wharf at Port Watsonville has felt the weight of the WR&N Co. electric cars, but still there is hope. Photograph courtesy Harold Van Gorder Collection

The Port Watsonville wharf stands solid in the surf. Photograph courtesy Pajaro Valley Historical Association

It has been over sixty-five years since the wharf at Port Watsonville saw its last ship. Today these storm-battered pilings are all that is left of a once-promising dream. Photograph courtesy Rick Hamman

of the first mortgage, brought suit, and the short-lived Watsonville Railway & Navigation Company was bankrupt. John E. Gardner was appointed receiver to liquidate the assets of the line. The rails were bought by the Southern Pacific, and the rolling stock went to various other concerns.

The creditors and stockholders received little return for the estimated $500,000 that had been swept away by repeated heavy seas and mismanagement during the railroad's ten years of existence. The attempt to create a seaport at Watsonville and compete with the Southern Pacific and the Pajaro Valley Consolidated had been an expensive and dismal failure.

The last attempt to revive the line was in 1915, when local citizens tried for federal aid to develop the port. The Congressional Rivers and Harbor Committee reviewed the site, made favorable comments, had a good time at the expense of the local people, and then departed, forgetting the matter forever.

IV / THE PAJARO VALLEY
CONSOLIDATED GLORY YEARS

Of Then, I Remember

UNABLE TO FIND EITHER significance or solace in my declining antiquity,
More and more I have returned to the Glory Years,
Now streaming comfortably together like silk and silver keepsakes,
Reflecting from the warm sunlit memories of the silent past.

I remember the seasons of pungent Salinas soil giving forth life,
First seeded and sown,
Then spaded and shoveled,
And finally, stript and stored.

I remember the sweet sugar beets, refinery style,
Delivered swollen and spongy,
Then sliced, steamed, saturated, strained, and eventually,
Turned into soft crystal sprinkles.

I remember the spheres of serene 1906 spring silence at Spreckels and Watsonville
and Moss Landing,
Suddenly surged and swayed,
Shocked and shaken,
Slumped and smashed.

I remember the stalwart sailing ships and steam powered schooners,
Guided by spars and spinnakers and sidewheels,
Skimming spiritedly across surf, spray, and sea,
Under schedule from the "Island" to San Francisco.

And most of all, I remember the little Pajaro Valley Consolidated,
With its slim steel rails straining staunchly under small gallant steeds,
Strongly stoked and spurred,
In spiritual sleekness.

William H. Anderson July 7, 1982

The day's events are over at Alisal Park. This time the picnic must have been attended by more funseekers than usual— a mogul is required to handle the boxcar, two coaches, and combine consist. Photograph courtesy Mrs. Carrie Hansen Collection

With the turn of the century and the beginning of what promised to be a new era of continuing growth and expansion for California and the Monterey Bay Area, the immediate future indeed seemed bountiful and glorious. Originally the Pajaro and Salinas valleys had been small agricultural regions where hard-working farmers and a few local businessmen had tried to eke out a living in support of each other. Then along came the Spreckels Sugar Company, and all of a sudden the fantastic sum of $2,000,000 a year was being spent locally. At the same time, the Pajaro Valley Consolidated brought increased wealth by providing local access to the entire West Coast via the Pacific Coast Steamship Company and other carriers at Moss Landing. In addition, the Southern Pacific Railroad was building south to Los Angeles, and all could envision the area being on the mainline of a north-south rail connection in the near future.

For the Pajaro Valley Consolidated, and for all shortline railroads across the country like it, this period would come to be known as the "Glory Years." It was a time when interstate highways, freeways, paved roads, and the automobiles, trucks, and buses that were to travel them were still transportation forms of the future. For now, the railroad was the prime mode of transportation for anybody and anything going anywhere. For the Pajaro Valley Consolidated, it meant not only transport of sugar beets before and after processing, but also grains, potatoes, various fruits and vegetables, building supplies, and people along the main. While the nearby Southern Pacific provided parallel service between Watsonville and Salinas, most locals used the Pajaro Valley Consolidated, as it better served the down-home country needs and attitudes of the local folks.

Between 1900 and 1915 the PVC, through the expansion of one branch and the construction of two others, reached its final system length of 42.2 miles. In addition to this mileage, there were fifty-four sidings, spurs, and passing tracks accounting for another 5.6 miles of rail on the ground. Adding the 5.0 miles of right-of-way belonging to the Watsonville Railway & Navigation Company, which actually became part of the PVC during a brief lease agreement in 1913, the narrow gauge railroads of Steinbeck Country during the Glory Years comprised 58.6 miles of active freight and passenger operations.

The following then is the story of the Pajaro Valley Consolidated narrow gauge railroad and the area it served in the Glory Years, before the rubber tire replaced the steel wheel.

The Branch Lines

ALISAL — the Alisal branch was originally constructed as part of the Pajaro Valley Extension Railroad in 1897 to meet the limestone needs of the Spreckels Sugar Company. Upon becoming part of the Pajaro Valley Consolidated, the branch was redesignated the "B" line, with the main from Spreckels to Watsonville being the "A" line. This "B" line began at a point known as Watsonville Junction 1.7 miles northeast of Spreckels and continued in a straight tangent for 5.1 miles across the rich Salinas Valley to the company's quarry in the Gabilan range foothills. The only obstacles it offered to construction and subsequent operation were those of a gradual grade extending from an elevation of 60 feet at the junction to 360 feet at the quarry, and the crossing at grade of the Southern Pacific's Spreckels branch and the Coast Route main.

Once the branch was in operation, it didn't take long for some of the enterprising young mischief-makers along the line to learn that empty cars on the upper end at the quarry could be operated by gravity almost all the way to the SP coast mainline crossing. Because of the obvious hazards involved, it soon became necessary, when spotting gondolas, for all train crews to chain and lock the lead downgrade cars to the track.

The problem of the SP Coast Route crossing, however, proved to be more of a headache than did the runaway cars. While the only service provided by the Pajaro Valley Consolidated over the branch was an irregular freight schedule, the possibility of a collision between a PVC and an SP train always loomed large. Even during the busy season when a signalman was posted at the crossing, neither railroad felt there was enough protection. As a result, in February of 1901

For over ninety years, various crews, using many different types of motive power, moved narrow and standard gauge freight cars around the Spreckels Sugar Company factory yards. This crew stopped late one afternoon during the early 1900s to help record this view for future generations. Photograph courtesy Monterey County Historical Society

plans were drawn up for the construction of an overcrossing above the SP mainline. The cost of the crossing was put at $6,671.05. Because the Alisal branch provided the Southern Pacific with a goodly amount of additional freight, they agreed to pay $2,000 of the total cost. The crossing included five and a quarter acres of new PVC right-of-way on which two trestles would be built, one twenty feet long and one forty feet long, with the curved approaches requiring over 27,000 cubic yards of fill. On April 14, 1901, J.B. McMahon & Son were awarded the contract, and by mid-July the overcrossing was completed and in service. Shortly after this, the grade crossing was removed by the SP and the materials shipped to the PVC at Spreckels. The PVC continuied to cross the SP Spreckels branch at grade.

Shortly after the completion of the overcrossing, an adjacent property owner filed a claim that stated that one of the PVC approaches infringed upon his property by eighteen feet and that the McMahon Company horses had eaten two tons of his hay during the course of construction. At a meeting with PVC General Manager Charles Pioda, the property owner (Mr. Johnson) was shown to his satisfaction that the railroad had not infringed upon his property. With respect to the hay, Mr. Pioda suggested that Mr. Johnson contact Mr. McMahon.

In October of 1901, a $3,400, 2,000-ton-capacity ware-house, 40 feet wide by 200 feet long, was erected by the PVC at the intersection of three county roads near the midpoint of the branch. This location is now at the juncture of Alisal and Bardin roads and the Bardin school grounds. It was from this centrally located point, to be known as Carr Station, that the railroad felt it could generate from six to eight thousand tons of barley and oat shipments yearly. The warehouse storage facilities and the railroad's interests were contractually looked after by the Ford & Sanborn Company, which rented the building for the sum of $22.60 per month.

In addition to the large acreages of hay and grains found along the Alisal branch, the area at the end of track in the hills east of Salinas was, and is, considered prime cattle country.

It was here that several feedlots, including those of the Spreckels Sugar Company Ranch #6 and the J. Bardin Ranch, were established to take care of the large bovine population. To keep these feedlots well supplied, the branch was extended 1.7 miles farther in 1902. This extension involved a consider-able amount of sidings and switches to serve the new feedlots.

During the sugar beet campaigns, beet pulp, long valued as an excellent cattle feed, was loaded into small four-wheel dump cars at Spreckels for shipment to the various cattle ranches along the branch. Later, a drying process was devel-oped, which both improved the quality of the pulp and its ease of handling. The dried pulp could be milled and warehoused, making it possible to space out shipments to the Alisal feedlots over the entire year. Beet pulp to this day is still con-sidered a very high quality cattle feed.

While freight was the main business of the PVC Alisal branch, there were also numerous occasions when an over-loaded passenger train wandered the "B" line rails. About a mile past the quarry the line happened to pass a point better known as Alisal Park. It was here that by 1902 a large dance floor and picnic grounds was built, much to the delight of all interested parties. Thus, the most popular of the PVC ex-cursions soon became the one to the park. The train would originate in Salinas and operate to Spreckels, where the loco-motive would run around the train for the trip out the Alisal branch to Alisal Park. What made the excursion so popular was the free barbecue thrown by the Spreckels Sugar Company. Besides this, dancing and games were always the order of the day. One young lady who used to attend the dances declared that the dance floor was mounted on springs and was constantly moving, but her husband said that it only seemed that way, because the more people there were, the more spring the floor had.

The park grounds were owned by the Spreckels Sugar Company and leased to the railroad. The dances and other festivities were usually sponsored by the Spreckels Volunteer Fire Department, which was made up of many of the sugar and railroad workers. Although the old-timers drank beer and

It's picnic time at Alisal Park. The ladies and gentlemen, boys and girls, are all gathered in their festive best, about to enjoy the trip out to the park and the day's activities. Photograph courtesy Monterey County Historical Society

always had a good time, they say that there was seldom
a problem with fights or vandalism.

The May Day and Sunday School picnics in particular
usually drew hundreds of adults and children. The fare for the
ride and entrance to the park was twenty-five cents. Due
to the ever-increasing size of the crowds, eventually the free
barbecue had to be ended, but attendance at the park remained high for many years.

All through the Glory Years the 6.8 mile Alisal branch of
the Pajaro Valley Consolidated Railroad functioned with
distinction. Thousands of tons of grains and other agricultural
products were transported to Moss Landing for ocean shipment, untold quantities of limestone crossed the Southern
Pacific Coast Route main on its way to the Spreckels sugar factory, and hundreds of carloads of beet pulp returned to the
feedlots. To accomplish all this, the company's proud little
2-6-0s carried the load, stopping briefly only at the lone water
tank between the quarry and Alisal Park.

*Many people have wandered along an infrequently used right-of-way
only to find that exact spot where a picture must be taken. So it must
have been on this particular day near the end of the Alisal branch.
Photograph courtesy John Hughes Collection, Monterey County
Historical Society*

SALINAS—with the failure and subsequent abandonment of the Salinas Railway Company in 1900, there was once again no satisfactory passenger transportation available between Salinas and Spreckels. There was also no direct connection either to Salinas or the Southern Pacific for the transfer of freight between lines. To resolve these problems, General Manager Pioda proposed that a new branch, the Salinas branch, be built between Spreckels and Salinas.

In 1908 a 2.2-mile line was surveyed from a point on the Alisal branch, to be known as Spreckels Junction, running parallel to and on the west side of the Southern Pacific Coast Route mainline, toward a proposed freight and passenger terminal in downtown Salinas. In a matter of a few months the new 4.7-mile Salinas branch had been started and completed, and freight and passenger service begun between the new terminal and Spreckels.

The Salinas terminal was located in a triangle formed by Monterey and Market streets on the northwest and southwest and the Southern Pacific tracks on the east. Its house track had a capacity of ten narrow gauge cars; the siding had a capacity of five cars. There were no oil or water facilities, or turntable. The single terminal building served as a combination freight shed, office, and passenger depot.

In addition to the Salinas depot, there was another small passenger shelter at the Alisal Street crossing behind the East End School. Also, there were three other station points on the branch that had spur tracks. They were Highway, Jeffrey, and Tynan (site of the present Tynan Lumber Company).

The majority of the revenue on the branch, with the exception of the United States mail, was from passenger service. The one-way fare between Salinas and the factory was fifteen cents, while the round trip went for two bits. During the yearly campaigns there were as many as nine passenger trains per day carrying seasonal workers between Salinas and Spreckels.

The regular locomotive used was the second No.1, a 2-4-2 saddle tank Baldwin. It was operated with an auxiliary tender to reduce the number of fuel and water stops. The tender was equipped with a pilot, since the locomotive was always operated from Salinas to Spreckels in reverse.

As mentioned previously, the Salinas Railway came just a little too soon, because the Salinas branch proved to be a real moneymaker for the Pajaro Valley Consolidated.

The PVC Depot at Salinas stands idle on this particular day. Photograph by Benny Romano

PVC No. 1 poses with crew at Spreckels to record an early view. Photograph courtesy Fred C. Stoes Collection

Pristine and stalwart, this handsome Mogul and its PVC crew pauses in time at Salinas to capture a glimpse of life during the Glory Years. Photograph courtesy Pajaro Valley Historical Association

The miniature Pajaro Valley Consolidated Mogul and its consist, waiting at the Salinas depot, seems small indeed when compared to the passing Southern Pacific standard gauge passenger train. Photograph courtesy John Hughes Collection, Monterey County Historical Society

September 7, 1914: The morning mixed for Salinas stands ready at Spreckels. Posing with the train are passengers and crew: Mr. W.T. Johnston, Mr. Collins, Fireman Foster, Engineer R.R. Weedon, and Mr. Grinnis. William Rosa stands alone by the combine in the background. Photograph courtesy Gilbert Kneiss Collection, Ted Wurm

PVC No. 7 is seen arriving at Salinas with one of the many daily commuter trains. Photograph courtesy University of California, Berkeley, Bancroft Library

BUENA VISTA – in 1898, shortly after the Spreckels factory had begun its operations, a new railroad spur was built south from the plant, across the Salinas River, and then west for about 100 yards along Buena Vista Road (now River Road) to the end of the track. Although the exact reasons for the construction of the spur are now lost to history, it is assumed that because there was no nearby river crossing, the Spreckels Sugar Company wanted better access for the PVC to its large land holdings on the southwestern side of the Salinas. Also, as an inducement to grow sugar beets, they wanted to provide the local area farmers on the opposite bank with a nearby freight-loading point.

Included in the construction of the spur was the erection of a curved, six-span truss bridge, the largest ever built for use by the railroad. The bridge itself was actually built and paid for by the Spreckels Sugar Company and then rented to the PVC railroad for $1,066.57 per year. This was because the source of cooling water for the factory power plant steam condensers was from large pumps set in about the middle of the Salinas River. To maintain these pumps and to remove them to safety during high water levels in the winter required the services of a standard gauge derrick on the bridge. As a result, this particular bridge had three rails for both standard and narrow gauge operation halfway across, and only narrow gauge rails to the end of the spur.

In 1901 a proposal was made to construct a new six-mile narrow gauge line along the west bank of the Salinas River from the spur in a southerly direction to the Spreckels Ranch on the old Buena Vista Spanish Rancho. During the previous campaign, over 9,000 tons of sugar beets had been shipped in by wagon from the area, and that was equivalent to over 900 carloads of narrow gauge freight. Because of this, it was the Spreckels Company–PVC intention to provide better transportation services to the ranch and to the rich agricultural lands found in the southern Salinas Valley. The proposal was initially rejected, however, as several farmers felt the branch was unnecessary. They also objected to the proposed route through their properties, since it would primarily serve the sugar company ranch lands.

In January of 1902, to appease the disgruntled farmers, the plan was modified with a proposal to only build a three-mile branch instead of the previously proposed six miles. The cost of the proposed right-of-way through nine parcels of land was put at $3,467.50, with the complete three-mile branch, including forty-five-pound rail, costing out at $35,301. Much to the dismay of the company, this plan too was met with stiff objections. As time went on, however, and more and more of farmers started growing sugar beets, the objections to the branch lessened. Thus, on April 19, 1905, the three-mile branch, with necessary sidings, was authorized by the Pajaro Valley Consolidated Railroad board of directors. The sum of $50,000 was allocated to cover the construction and any other contingencies that might arise. In short order, the Buena Vista, or "C," branch was in operation.

Soon the Buena Vista branch was extended to its original six-mile proposed length, and plans were put forth to extend it even farther. This, however, never happened, and the branch remained six miles long over its entire life.

Technically, the Buena Vista branch started at a switch on the southern approach to the Salinas River Bridge. Because the bridge curved to the southwest, toward the end of the original spur, instead of to the southeast, in the direction of the Buena Vista Ranch, all trains crossing the river had to first clear the switch and fill the spur and then proceed through the switch in the opposite direction. Trains coming into the factory encountered the same problem in reverse.

Located a short distance from the branch switch and the bridge was the first spur, known as Corey Station. This nineteen-car spur served gravel quarry No. 1 on the branch, which was used during the initial construction to supply roadbed fill. Later, quarry materials were extracted to help build levees along the north side of the Salinas River to protect the factory from winter floods.

From Corey Station, the railroad continued south along the river for about a half-mile to the Armstrong Brothers

Sunday afternoon, January 25, 1914: The Salinas River is rising to an all-time high. This is perhaps the last view ever taken of the original alignment on the Buena Vista branch, for by the following morning the three near spans would be gone and the west approach to the bridge forever changed. Photograph courtesy Miss Rose Rhyner, Spreckels Sugar Co. Collection

The company's famous weed-burner car is seen situated along the Buena Vista branch, first with PVC crew and then in action. Photograph courtesy Miss Rose Rhyner, Spreckels Sugar Co. Collection

A closeup look at the end of the Buena Vista branch. Photograph courtesy University of California, Berkeley, Bancroft Library

Ranch, where a large spur had been put down at a place called Armstrong. At the end of the spur there was a ninety-degree curve of portable light track, which entered the ranch. This track was used to deliver beet pulp for cattle feed. The light track was not considered part of the spur and locomotives were not allowed to operate on it.

Continuing south, the line wandered from section to section for the next two and a half miles, passing through the Hill and Laymon places, until it finally reached Seegeiken. It was here, originally the end of the three-mile line, that the only passing siding on the branch was to be found. As a result, locomotives would always be run around their respective trains at this point for the trip back to Spreckels. Locomotives were normally operated tender first outbound so that they would be on the head end of the loaded trains returning to the factory.

A short distance from Seegeiken, at Agenda, stood the only water tank to be found on the entire branch. It was also here, in the middle of the Spreckels Buena Vista Ranch, that the largest spur on the PVC, having a capacity of sixty-six sugar beet cars, began. To fill these cars, a mammoth beet loading station at Thygisen, located at the opposite end of the 2,000-foot spur, was in constant operation during each campaign. One-half mile beyond Agenda the company had begun working another quarry, known as No.2, where a 1,100-foot spur led into more privately owned portable track. From here, it was a short mile and a quarter to the end of track at Buena Vista Terminal.

As shortline railroads go, the Buena Vista branch didn't meet with many problems either in construction or subsequent operation. The branch, climbing only twenty-four feet in six miles between Corey at sixty-three feet and Buena Vista at eighty-seven feet, was essentially level. It had just nine spurs and passing sidings, and all switches entered from the west except for an eastern entrance at Corey. There was no major trestling required, as the branch only had two bridges, one two-section, 32 feet long by 9 feet high, and one seven-section, 112 feet long by 16 feet high. Finally, as the track was only a single mainline used for irregular and seasonal freight, no

heavy maintenance and upkeep was necessary.

In January of 1914, during the peak of the winter rainy season, an extremely intense storm began to hammer California and Steinbeck Country in particular. It wasn't long before the Salinas River became a raging collection of muddy water on the rampage, removing almost every man-made obstacle in its way. Included in this earthly movement were the southern three sections of the bridge from the factory to the Buena Vista branch.

Sometimes from a disaster comes the reasons and the means for a new and better beginning. So it was for the Salinas River Bridge; not once, as planned, but twice, because of the railroad's worst tragedy.

After the rains and the flood waters had subsided, and the Salinas River had returned to its usual mere surface trickle, with the bulk of the Monterey Bay-bound flow running underground, reconstruction of the bridge began. This time the bridge was built much stronger, with concrete piers instead of wooden supports, thus allowing for a 100-ton per section loading. Also, to better serve the Buena Vista branch, the three washed-out sections were reconstructed in a curve toward the southeast instead of the southwest.

By the time the new structure was completed in early September, it had developed a definite "S" shape. In addition, the bridge's southern approach and the parallel county road had been realigned, and the trackage southwest of the bridge had been removed. In short order, heavily laden sugar beet trains once again began to cross the new bridge, bound for the factory with the previous campaign's production.

On October 23, 1914, Mr. H.R. Smith, who had been in the Salinas area for only about a week, came to the Spreckels Sugar Company seeking gainful employment. His reported credentials were that he had recently been working on a railroad construction project in Humbolt County and that he was in need of a job. That afternoon he was hired and was immediately put to work in the company railroad yard doing odd jobs.

The next morning, October 24th, the maintenance boss

Above, empty gondolas line the Gravel Pit No. 2 siding waiting to be filled. Right, gondola is about to be filled, while to the far right the bucket has unloaded. Photographs courtesy Amstar, Spreckels Collection

January 26, 1914. Severe winter storms off the Pacific Ocean have turned the underground Salinas River into a raging surface torrent. Above, a side view of the remaining bridge to the Buena Vista branch is pictured. Right, the Salinas River can be seen as it pounds the bridge. Following page, unable to stay within its previous boundaries, the Salinas River has left its banks and is raising havoc with the countryside. Photographs courtesy Miss Rose Rhyner, Spreckels Sugar Co. Collection

Levee at Spreckels. Flood 1914.

put Mr. Smith and three other handymen out on the southern-most section of the Salinas River Bridge to finish up the last portion of painting. As the day wore on and the tedium of painting the bridge began to overtake Smith and the other workers, the approach of engine No.6 with its heavy sugar beet train coming off the Buena Vista branch no doubt momentarily broke the monotony of the day. Slowly the train, with Engineer Jones at the throttle and Fireman Baldwin working the boiler, began to make the eastern curve toward the first 200-foot bridge section, which Smith and the other painters were on. Smith could see Conductor Green and one of the brakemen standing on the forward cars with Brakeman Lauritzen positioned about six cars back from the engine. As the train moved onto the first span Smith paused to count the cars; one, two, three, four . . . suddenly the span began to shake and shudder, concrete was cracking, wooden beams were splintering, steel was buckling, everything was coming apart; all at once the bridge, the train, and all things connected to them began to collapse.

That was Mr. Smith's last sight: engine No.6, its crew, and the first six cars all crashing into the riverbed below along with the jumbled remains of the first bridge section. Mr. Smith was the only fatality of this horrible tragedy.

The others involved in the accident received various broken bones and internal injuries. In addition, Engineer Jones and Fireman Baldwin not only received similar injuries, but they were also trapped in the cab of the locomotive for some time, where they suffered some very painful and very severe burns. Eventually, help arrived, and everyone was removed from the wreckage and sent to waiting ambulances in Salinas via special train. Fortunately, Jay Lauritzen, the rear brakeman, saw that the car he was riding on was going to end up in the debris, and he jumped into some willows, escaping unhurt.

At the hearing into the accident, testimony of witnesses indicated that the train had proceeded for 160 feet onto the first span when it collapsed without warning. The span had previously been in service since early September without any notice of undue vibration or fault. It was supposedly designed to withstand a train of 100 tons plus a safety factor, and the the train involved was estimated to weigh only 80 tons. There were several theories as to why the span collapsed, including one that the train had approached at too high a speed, and that centrifugal force had dislodged the span. The wreckage was inspected by the designer/contractor, the Merry Elwell Company of Oakland, which concluded that one of the steel casting supports had failed. There was also an inspection by the State Railroad Commission, but there is no record of any verdict. One thing is certain, the combination wood and steel span had failed. Since the Buena Vista branch was to continue, it was replaced by a new and even stronger all-steel structure that would far outlast the railroad.

As for H.R. Smith, the man who was in the wrong place at the wrong time, no one ever stepped forward to claim his remains, so he was buried in Salinas, where he rests to this day.

Above, the engine, cars, and bridge lie in joint rubble while right, the wrecked engine is pictured by itself, lying on its side like a wounded animal. Photographs courtesy Amstar, Spreckels Sugar Co. Collection

People stand around in disbelief as they view a fallen bridge and a demolished train. Photograph courtesy Miss Rose Rhyner, Spreckels Sugar Co. Collection

Spreckels: the factory, the town, the railroad, and the brand new Salinas River Bridge to the Buena Vista branch.
Photograph courtesy Amstar, Spreckels Collection

The Seaport – Moss Landing

The Monterey & Salinas Valley Railroad was originally incorporated to try to connect the vast Salinas Valley farmlands and the City of Salinas with the reputable California seaport of Monterey. The idea behind the incorporation was to provide the area farmers and ranchers with better access to a larger market and to offer through passenger service to prominent points up and down the Pacific Coast. Because of stiff competition, poor planning, and a lot of bad luck, the execution of the idea was initially short lived. A few years later the Pajaro Valley Consolidated Railroad came along with connections to Watsonville and Salinas, worked out a long-term agreement with the Pacific Coast Steamship Company at Moss Landing, and an old idea was given new life.

Today if one looks at the harbor of Moss Landing, with its fleet of 200 commercial fishing boats and its many and varied pleasure craft, one finds it hard to believe that such an operation as the PVC–PCSS Co. ever existed. But exist it did.

The steamship company facilities at Moss Landing were quite extensive. They included a 406-foot bridge across the Salinas River between the mainland and their wharf on the Island, four large warehouses, each 65 feet by 300 feet, stables for their workhorses, company offices, monstrous scales, yard trackage, and equipment necessary to serve the needs of the port.

The bridge, thirty feet south of and running parallel to the PVC bridge, was twenty-four feet wide and had decking and narrow gauge trackage so that both horsedrawn wagons and railroad cars could be operated across it. The bridge was completely fenced, with a locked gate positioned on the mainland end. Warehouse No.1 was located on the Island end of the bridge just to the south of the trackage leading onto the wharf. Warehouses No.2 and No.3 sat adjacent to warehouse No.1 except on the north side of the wharf trackage. Warehouse No.4 was situated on the mainland. The trackage on the bridge connected the mainland warehouse with the Island warehouses and the wharf.

There was double track on the wharf, with a short spur on a finger pier at the shoreline. PVC locomotives were allowed to operate only on the railroad's wye and Salinas River trestle, on the track leading into warehouse No.4 from the mainline, and on a short spur adjacent to warehouse No.1. They did not operate on the wharf or the parallel steamship company bridge. All PVC car movements on PCSS Co. property trackage was accomplished with horses.

In addition to PVC rolling stock on the property, the steamship company had a number of its own cars, which were used between the warehouses and the wharf. These were small, four-wheeled, one- or two-horse drawn cars, each capable of handling 250 sacks of grain. Also, as barge traffic on the Salinas River and connecting sloughs was still very much a way of life, a derrick was positioned on the steamship company bridge to transfer freight from barge to railcar to the appropriate warehouse.

It should be remembered here that all during the early portion of the Glory Years, from 1900 until 1906, the Salinas River emptied into Monterey Bay about a half-mile north of Moss Landing. Thus, the river and the nearby interconnecting Moro Cojo and Elkhorn sloughs all formed a small inland bay, which, in effect, cut off the wharf and warehouse area from the mainland. The "Island" on which they were situated was actually a small peninsula about 100 feet to 600 feet across and approximately two miles long, which separated the Salinas River from Monterey Bay.

Perhaps at this juncture mention should be made of just where all the PVC–PCSS Co. freight was coming from and exactly what its makeup was. First and foremost, the reader should not be lulled into believing, based on the foregoing text, that sugar and the sugar beet was the primary crop of the Pajaro and Salinas valleys. While sugar was the largest cash crop at over $2,000,000 annually, it certainly wasn't the most land consumptive. The raising of beets involved only about 20,000 acres of land, whereas the growing of barley and wheat consumed over 150,000 acres of prime valley properties and generated its own $1,250,000 of gross income. Also, about

The Gipsy *is under way. Photograph courtesy Fred C. Stoes Collection*

The Moss Landing wharf is very busy on this day as steam and sail powered ships line the dock. Photograph courtesy Monterey County Historical Society

Boxcars and grain cars line the Moss Landing wharf as the Gipsy *transfers freight. During the Glory Years the wharf, as pictured here, was substantial enough in length and structure to accommodate almost any size ship. Photograph courtesy Albert Vierra Collection*

In this rare view, looking toward shore and the Island, the sails have been lashed into place and the rigging attended to. Soon the ship will be brought alongside the wharf. Photograph courtesy Monterey County Historical Society

5,000 acres were devoted to the Salinas Burbank potato, which accounted for another $1,500,000 yearly. And the Watsonville apple of the Pajaro Valley was responsible for an additional $1,000,000.

A combination of all these products created the joint PVC-PCSS Co. freight that continually arrived at Moss Landing. From the Salinas Valley came large shipments of barley, grain, and potatoes, with smaller shipments of beans, onions, and peas in carload lots. From the Pajaro Valley came apples and other fruit, dairy products and produce.

After the various narrow gauge branches had been completed, and the PVC had begun direct service to Salinas, the railroad's business soon increased so much that a new 40 percent railroad–60 percent steamship company through tariff split was easily renegotiated. One through waybill was issued for both incoming and outgoing freight, and the accounts of the two companies were settled at the end of each month. The balance of payments was usually in favor of the steamship company. Freight could be stored at the warehouses for a designated length of time before a new waybill had to be issued. As the warehouses were owned by the steamship company, they received all the fees for warehousing.

For many years Mr. S.N. Laughlin, the steamship company agent at Moss Landing, kept a very accurate accounting of all shipments and transactions between the two companies and the shippers. Any discrepancy in weights or claims not attended to within a reasonable time by the railroad agents at Watsonville or Salinas were immediately referred directly to the railroad superintendent for action. Complaints and claims for damages were handled in the same manner. Once it was determined which company was responsible, the claim was immediately settled, although usually not in the amount the shipper suggested.

Overall, the Southern Pacific was suprisingly cooperative with the Pajaro Valley Consolidated–Pacific Coast Steamship Company operation, even to the point of keeping them informed of any rate changes so the combination could adjust their rates accordingly. The narrow gauge–steamship rate to

San Francisco from Watsonville and Salinas was held slightly lower than the SP rate, even though it required a transfer at Moss Landing. On several occasions the SP lowered their rate while the PVC did not, and the PVC immediately heard from their shippers.

The Pajaro Valley Consolidated would then adjust their rate and make an allowance to the shipper. In most cases the steamship company held their rate, and any lowering of rates had to be done by the PVC. Usually the PVC turned down requests made by a particular shipper for a special rate if the PVC felt that granting such a rate would upset their relationship with the Southern Pacific.

The PCSS Co. operated six primary routes along the Pacific Coast. Included in these were the Narrow Gauge Route and the San Francisco–Monterey Overnighter, which served Moss Landing. The Narrow Gauge Route called at many ports, including San Francisco, Santa Cruz, Monterey, San Simeon, Cayucos, Port Harford, Lompoc Landing, Gaviota, Santa Barbara, Ventura, Hueneme, San Pedro, and Newport Landing, while the Overnighter operated locally.

The regular ship on the Overnighter was the 239-ton steam schooner *Gipsy*, affectionately known as "Old Perpetual Motion." The *Gipsy* usually left San Francisco Tuesday and Friday mornings at 9:00 A.M. and by the following Wednesday and Saturday afternoons had cleared the Port of Santa Cruz and was docking at Moss Landing. From Moss Landing Old Perpetual Motion went on to Monterey and then returned to San Francisco, where the trip started all over again.

After over fifteen years of on-time and continuous service, the *Gipsy* met a rather inglorious end. On the evening of September 27, 1905, the ship left Moss Landing for Monterey, after having loaded approximately $15,000 worth of mixed cargo, under the command of relief captain Thomas Boyd. At 8:00 P.M. Captain Boyd sighted the channel buoy off Monterey and altered course to enter the harbor. Through the dense fog Captain Boyd saw the glow of a red light, which he believed to be the marker at the end of the Monterey wharf. Only a few minutes had passed after altering course before a warning

A four-masted schooner is moored at the end of the wharf. Photograph courtesy Pajaro Valley Historical Association

rang out from the lookout, "Breakers ahead." Before the ship could be stopped or brought about it crashed into the rocks off MacAbee Beach and immediately started to take on water. The crew, forced to abandon ship in the lifeboats, soon thereafter watched from shore as the gallant *Gipsy* was battered into oblivion.

The marker light that had led the ship to its final destruction was later found to be nothing more than a red lantern at a sewer project near the end of Hoffman Street in Monterey.

Although the Pacific Coast Steamship Company was the prime oceangoing carrier operating out of Moss Landing, there were several other independent companies making direct connection with the PVC at the port. Among them were the South Coast Steamship Company and the Dollar Steamship Lines.

Upon the completion of the Panama Canal, the Dollar Line started to call at Moss Landing during the harvesting season with two large steel-hulled ships to load shiever barley for direct shipment to Germany. The shiever barley was a very hard grain that didn't have the stiff beard of common barley and looked more like wheat. The Germans prized this grain grown in semiarid conditions for the flavor it gave their many first-class beers. Most of the shiever barley was grown in the upper Salinas Valley, shipped from there by the Southern Pacific to Salinas, and then loaded aboard special PVC trains and transported to Moss Landing. The barley was usually bagged in 120- to 125-pound sacks, and it took two men to move them from place to place.

During the height of the grain season other special Pajaro Valley Consolidated freight trains were operated from the Pajaro and Salinas valleys to Moss Landing. On several occasions there were as many as six or seven steam schooners waiting their turn to tie up to the wharf for loading. The grain trains would arrive at Moss Landing, set out the loaded cars and perform any required switching. The engine would then be turned on the wye, couple onto the empty string of cars, and head back toward Salinas. Grain that arrived for direct shipment was sent out on the wharf in the PVC cars. The wharf had

two parallel tracks with a crossover for the convenience of car movements by the teams of horses. In addition to normal mixed service, there was usually a scheduled local that operated between Salinas and Moss Landing during the busy seasons. Longtime Moss Landing resident William Lehman remembers cutting high school many times to earn fifty cents a day loading the grain ships.

The Moss Landing warehouses were preferred over the warehouses in the Salinas Valley because the dry grain gained weight during storage there. Since the warehouses were built on piles over water, the grain would absorb moisture from the air. Usually the farmers let their grain sit in the warehouses until they thought they could get the best price possible.

They had a long-standing joke at Moss Landing about a farmer named Pat Ryan. It seems farmer Ryan had contacted the steamship company agent, Mr. Laughlin, concerning bulk warehouse space available, quantity storage, and volume shipping rates. After pondering the situation for some time, Ryan delivered three sacks of grain for storage. Mr. Laughlin later inquired as to when he might expect the rest of the grain, and Ryan informed him that three sacks was all he intended to warehouse and ship. Three sacks of grain in a 65-foot by 300-foot warehouse was somewhat less than a bulk shipment.

While Moss Landing was primarily a PVC freight-generating revenue station, it did occasionally serve passenger functions. One such function was the yearly narrow gauge excursion affectionately referred to as the "Boxcar Picnic." In this case two separate trains were operated from Salinas and Watsonville. It gave friends and relatives from both towns an opportunity to meet and visit and to get in a little fishing and beach activity.

The Pacific Coast Steamship Company's coastal steamer Coos Bay *is departing Moss Landing for Monterey and San Francisco. Photograph courtesy Pajaro Valley Historical Association*

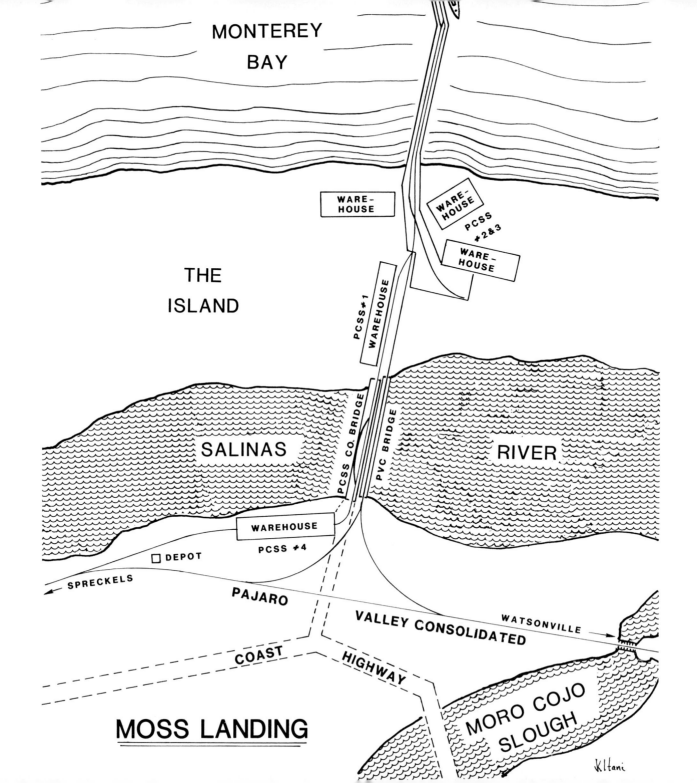

MONTEREY
BAY

THE
ISLAND

WARE-HOUSE

WARE-HOUSE
PCSS #2 & 3

WARE-HOUSE

PCSS #1
WAREHOUSE

PCSS CO. BRIDGE

PVC BRIDGE

SALINAS

RIVER

WAREHOUSE

PCSS #4

DEPOT

SPRECKELS

PAJARO

VALLEY CONSOLIDATED

WATSONVILLE

COAST   HIGHWAY

MOSS LANDING

MORO COJO
SLOUGH

K. Itani

Flatcars loaded with grain await shipment from Moss Landing. Photograph courtesy University of California, Berkeley, Bancroft Library

Grain is being loaded from a lighter onto waiting Pacific Coast Steamship Company cars for final transhipment to a company steamer. Photograph courtesy Monterey County Historical Society

Naturally the wharf at Moss Landing saw uses other than shipping. Above, several people are fishing in the surf for perch and flounder, while to the right, a group of ladies pose on a PCSS Co. grain car during a Sunday afternoon outing. Photographs courtesy Pajaro Valley Historical Association

Disasters, Tragedies, and Comedies

THE EARTHQUAKE — on the morning of April 18, 1906, the worst earthquake ever to be recorded in California struck the San Francisco and Monterey Bay areas. After the land underfoot had stopped gyrating, and the horrible moans and rumblings coming from deep within the earth had ceased, devastation, to a greater or lesser degree, was found everywhere.

Prior to the earthquake, the Salinas River had emptied into Monterey Bay just north of Moss Landing. By the time the earthquake was over, the sand spit between the river and the bay, the Island, had gone through a tremendous uplifting and had moved several feet to the east. This caused several changes in the tidal basin and the Salinas River channel. Among them, the mouth of the river was immediately sealed off and a new mouth instantly created two miles south of Moss Landing at what had been, until then, a secondary outlet. There is still some controversy over whether the earthquake itself caused the changes, or whether the earthquake and some slower natural changes, such as local farmers repeatedly opening a channel during the rainy season through the secondary outlet to prevent flooding, were responsible. Either way, it happened. Fortunately, the channel was squeezed at Mulligan Hill, but still left open as far as Moss Landing.

Some of the worst damage sustained was to the Pacific Coast Steamship Company facilities and the Pajaro Valley Consolidated Railroad trackage at Moss Landing. With the eastward movement of the Island, the two trestles were set askew and the rail on them buckled. On the Island one warehouse completely collapsed and several railroad cars were knocked off their trucks. Between Moro Cojo and Moss Landing the PVC tracks shifted several inches in places, while north of Moss Landing the roadbed settled nearly two feet at several of the slough crossings.

Damage along the Pajaro River was confined to the shifting of the roadbed and minor movement of the Pajaro River Bridge approaches. The roadbed near the mouth of the Pajaro River was reported to have shifted twelve feet to the northeast.

The town of Spreckels received very little damage, but at the factory the brick walls of the main building were buckled and displaced, heavy machinery and piping was torn loose, and the water reservoir was partially destroyed.

A fuel oil pipeline from Coalinga to Monterey, which also served the factory and the railroad, was broken where it crossed the Salinas River at the Monterey Road crossing. In all, the line was broken in twenty places in the Salinas Valley area. The pipe was found to be three feet apart in places, while there was an overlap of four feet in other locations. Oddly enough, the pipeline was said to be undamaged where it crossed the San Andreas Fault.

In spite of all the damage sustained, the railroad was able to resume normal operations within a few days. The PCSS Co. and the Spreckels Sugar Company were likewise in operation shortly thereafter.

The earthquake of 1906 is over, and the office above has moved to the right of its original location, which is marked by the stake. Photograph courtesy United States Geological Survey, Menlo Park, California

The damage sustained by the Spreckels Sugar Company factory was substantial. Above, the end of the main building is in disarray, and a look down the side shows a wall bulging slightly. To the right, the Steffins building is likewise in need of some major brick work. Photographs courtesy Amstar, Spreckels Collection

Above, in this view looking out to sea, the PCSS Co. Island area is in total chaos. To the left, more earthquake damage is witnessed in this picture looking inland, off the end of the wharf. Photographs courtesy Amstar, Spreckels Collection

April 18, 1906. Earthquake damage at Moss Landing is the subject of these views. Photographs courtesy United States Geological Survey, Menlo Park, California

THE PREMONITIONS – the twenty-first day of January 1900 was a rather cool and blustery winter Sunday. As a result, Cyrus Wyckoff, his wife Isabel, and their three sons moved along briskly as they made their way to the evening services at the Christian Church of Watsonville.

Cyrus Wyckoff and his fast-growing family had lived in the Watsonville area for the last ten years, ever since he had first gone to work for the Pajaro Valley Railroad. At thirty-five years of age Cyrus had become the company's first locomotive engineer, earning the then goodly salary of $3.33 per day. Now, at forty-five, he was first in seniority, having worked aboard every locomotive and over every foot of track the PVC owned. He was well liked by his fellow railroad workers and the people along the line, and he was regarded as an upstanding member of the Watsonville community and of his church.

On hand to greet the Wyckoffs as they arrived for church was the minister, R.H. Sawyer. After the normal pleasantries had been exchanged and the day's events briefly discussed, the conversation seemed to trail off. For some unexplained reason Rev. Sawyer seemed to be ill at ease. Sensing the odd feelings of the moment, the Wyckoffs politely broke off the conversation and entered the church. Soon thereafter the service began.

As the minister began his sermon he could not shake a feeling of depression and morbidness that had troubled him ever since the Wyckoffs had arrived. Now and then he lost his train of thought. Several times his words became confused and ran together. Finally, he lost total consciousness of the point he was trying to make and paused to regain his composure. Suddenly, he saw the face of an unidentified dead man appear in front of him and felt deeply the loss of a dear friend. In an instant the feeling was gone and the rest of the sermon and the night went without incident. All the members, including the Wyckoffs, were aware of the minister's faltering sermon that evening, but custom dictated silence.

7:00 A.M. Monday morning, January 22, 1900. The Wyckoffs had already finished breakfast. The children were now putting on clothes, gathering school books, and getting ready for the day. Isabel was out in the kitchen adding the finishing touches to her husband's lunch while he was getting ready to leave for work. Cyrus paused as he entered her warm working space. He gazed for a few moments at his wife of many years, gathering up his favorite memories of her in his mind and savoring each for a microsecond. All at once he startled Isabel by pulling her to him and smothering her with lingering and loving kisses.

After a few seconds his wife looked into his eyes, beyond their physical limits, and sensed a nervousness within him that she had never seen before. She asked him in a very concerned and caring manner what was wrong. He replied that he felt depressed and nervous, as though some kind of fatality hung over him. Knowing that he was a very careful and safety-conscious person, she tried to cheer him up by laughing it off, citing the cause as the coldness of the morning and the gray dampness of the day. With that they parted, she to return to her usual Monday chores and he to govern the throttle aboard engine No.4 on the head end of Mixed No.1 between Watsonville and Spreckels.

7:15 A.M., a cold, dense, wintry fog hung over the Pajaro and Salinas valleys and the PVC Watsonville railroad yard in particular. Visibility was next to nothing. As Cyrus Wyckoff walked out to board engine No.4 and begin making up the 8:00 A.M. mixed for Spreckels, he found the early morning atmosphere strangely in tune with his uneasy state of mind. Try as he might, he couldn't shake off his eerie feelings of impending doom. Even the friendly interchange of greetings and waves between Conductor Field, leaving on freight No.3, and himself didn't seem to relax the tension. "Oh well," Wyckoff rationalized, "maybe my wife was right." Freight train No.5 had left about 6:30 A.M., and now train No.3 was out. That put two trains ahead of him on the main in the fog. If something went wrong either conductor on those trains would certainly call the dispatcher and report any problems.

Because the PVC was continually blessed with coastal fog, winter washouts and flooding, and livestock on the right-of-way, Superintendent Waters had inaugurated the use of the telephone, coupled with the telegraph, to insure better train dispatching and safety. It is said to have been the first railroad in the country to do so. In addition to the station phones, each train was equipped with a wire-hook-tipped wooden pole and a portable telegraph key set. To communicate with the dispatcher, the crew simply stopped the train so the conductor could attach a wire from the metal tip of the pole, which was hooked on the telegraph line, to the sending key, and a wire from the key to the rail. In this fashion the circuit was completed and communications between train and dispatcher could take place anywhere along the line at any time. So far this system had proved to be very successful.

7:40 A.M., Gaffey's Switch, north entrance to the twenty-four-car Cooper Ranch siding, fifteen miles southwest of Watsonville. Tenant farmer James Larkin and his fifteen-year-old son had just arrived at the siding from the fields with their first wagonload of sugar beets for the day to be dumped into waiting PVC gondolas. They paused by the water tank to watch freight train No.5, with its long string of beet cars, clear the switch and slowly grope its way through the early morning fog along the invisible right-of-way to Spreckels.

8:00 A.M., Pajaro Valley Consolidated Railroad Terminal, Watsonville. Train No.1 was sitting ready to leave for Spreckels. This morning's consist behind locomotive No.4 included an empty boxcar, nine loaded gondolas, and the combination baggage-passenger coach. The train's crew was the usual Engineer Wyckoff and Fireman Green in the cab, brakemen Tucker and Sanborn riding in the empty boxcar to avoid the cold, and Conductor Huff, along with seven pasengers, occupying the combination coach. Conductor Huff and Engineer Wyckoff had both started out on the first train many years ago. Since then, they had worked many trains together and had become good friends in the process. Conductor Huff from somewhere back in the fog yelled the familiar "Bo-o-a-r-d," Engineer Wyckoff released the brakes on the engine, and the little narrow gauge train began its typical morning sojourn through Steinbeck Country to Spreckels.

8:20 A.M., Gaffey's Switch, freight train No.3 had just cleared the switch and had momentarily come to a stop in front of the water tank. It was here, at the Cooper Ranch siding, that train No.3 was required to enter the hole and wait for mixed train No.1 to pass from behind. This was because mixed train No.1 had prioritiy over any freight train on the main. On this particular morning the freight train would have to back into the 850-foot siding from the south, since the north end was filled with empty beet cars waiting to be loaded. While the forward brakeman went ahead to throw the lower switch, Conductor Field ambled over to where James Larkin and his son were loading beet cars. When the train had first passed the Larkins, he thought he had seen them putting up a block and tackle on a telegraph pole. This was a practice not allowed by the PVC, so he wanted to bring it to their attention. Sure enough, rather than use the deadman post as required, James Larkin was about to string a heavy seven-eighths cable across the PVC mainline and attach it to a tele-graph pole. Conductor Field soon put a stop to that tomfoolery.

To facilitate the unloading of beets from wagons, a strong net was placed in the bottom of the wagon and draped over the sides and ends. For unloading, the wagon was driven along-side a railroad car at the nearest siding. A block and tackle was then attached to a deadman post between the siding and the mainline on the opposite side of the rail car from the wagon. The line was carried over the car to the far side of the net on the wagon, the near side of the net being attached to the rail car side. A team of horses was then secured to the running line of the block and tackle to lift the load out of the wagon and into the railroad car. All the farmers along the railroad had been notified repeatedly not to fasten their lines to telegraph poles or tracks, but to use the deadman posts provided.

With the Larkins taken care of, Conductor Field returned to his train to make sure it got into the lower end of the siding. The last thing he wanted was for his train to be on the main in the fog when the mixed arrived. By the time train No.1 was due to arrive, the freight was positioned on the siding at the lower end and the main was clear.

8:50 A.M., two miles west of the Moro Cojo Ranch, mixed

train No. 1 was approaching the flag stop of Gaffey's Switch, now known as Cooper. Engineer Wyckoff peered down the side of his slim Baldwin steed, straining his eyes through the dense fog in search of continued footing. The ground moisture was so thick that the train seemed to be traveling in a void separated from time and space. About a half-mile from the Cooper flag stop the steam was shut off and the heavy sugar beet and passenger mixed gradually began to slow. Cyrus Wyckoff reached up and grabbed the whistle cord and began piercing the silence to let any and all know the train was approaching. Fireman Green, like his engineer, started searching the veiled horizon for movement from any form, be it beast in the way or man waiting to board the combine, now seventeen cars back. Little by little the train decreased speed until it was gently drifting along at ten miles per hour.

The switch was barely seen and past. No one was present. Engineer Wyckoff laid on the whistle cord once more to indicate same to the invisible conductor somewhere back in the fog. Ever so carefully, the locomotive was given just a little steam to propel it and its heavy train farther down the line. Soon, the caboose on freight train No. 3 was due to be seen on the passing track at the other end of the Cooper siding.

All at once the water tank loomed in the mist, and an eerie shiver of subconscious instinct and cold pierced the engine cab and those within it. Without warning, the sound and the fury of metal binding and crushing metal was heard and felt. Wyckoff screamed at Green, "We've hit something! The front truck is off the track and the pilot is digging into the ties and the ground ahead of us!" Green retorted in fear, "Reverse the wheels, reverse the wheels!" Wyckoff reached out and pulled on the reverse lever, but the weight of the train behind him was too great. In fleeting desperation he grabbed the whistle cord and signaled "On Brakes." The engine began to oscillate. Metal gnashed against metal. Futilely, Wyckoff and Green both leaned on the reverse lever to try to slow their wavering mount. Unfortunately, their efforts were to no avail. Suddenly, the rail comprising the southern switch of Cooper siding was struck by the pilot. The engine rose straight up

in the air like a wounded animal, pivoted about a point, shuddered and shook, and then began to tip over on its side. As the iron horse was going down, the force on the drivers pulled the reverse lever from Fireman Green, throwing him out of the cab. The lever then sprang straight at Cyrus Wyckoff, piercing his body through the heart. The Baldwin lay helpless, clawing at the ground with its wheels still under power, gyrating in uncomfortable bursts of energy and anguish.

Once everything had stopped moving and shaking, Conductor Huff came forward to survey the damage. To his horror he found Engineer Wyckoff still hanging on the reverse lever, pinned between the side of the cab, which had been crushed, and the boiler. It was almost two hours before the Johnson Bar could be sawn through and Engineer Wyckoff's body removed to a waiting passenger car.

Fireman Green had been more fortunate. He had sailed through the air for about fifteen feet and had landed in a large pool of mud, receiving only minor injuries. Brakemen Tucker and Sanborn, who had been riding in the boxcar immediately behind the tender, were found more scared than hurt. As the accident was happening, the boxcar had reared up in the air, the brakemen were catapulted to its end, the outside doors slammed shut, and the car came back down, completely clear of the track. Then the three following beet cars smashed into the boxcar, significantly damaging it and totally demolishing them. Fortunately, the brakemen had been thrown into a portion of the car that did not sustain much damage. As a result, while it took a little time to remove them from the wreckage, they were unharmed. The passengers in the combine were only slightly shaken up and were able to help in the rescue work.

Conductor Huff telegraphed the news of the accident to Spreckels and Watsonville, and a wrecking crew, with Superintendent Waters and the Monterey County coroner, were soon on the scene. Mrs. Wyckoff received the news less than two hours after bidding her husband goodbye. This was the the only accident on the PVC in which an on-board crew member lost his life.

How did it happen? At the coroner's inquest the following answer came to light. After Conductor Field on train No.3 had told farmer Larkin to unhook his block and tackle, and had then gone on down to the end of the siding, Larkin put it right back. He thus unloaded his beets into one of the gondolas and returned with his son to the fields three-quarters of a mile away for another load. But he had forgotten to remove the steel hook attached to the rail and the seven-eighths inch steel cable strung across the mainline. Because it was foggy, Engineer Wyckoff could not see the track. As a result, the pony truck struck the hook, cut the cable in two, and jumped the track. The train then proceeded in this fashion down the line for 170 feet until striking the switch. The horrifying part of it for farmer Larkin was that when he first heard the whistle at Gaffey's Switch, he immediately knew what was going to happen, but was powerless to prevent it.

To keep such a thing from ever happening again, the railroad later built elevated beet dumps. The wagon went up a ramp beside the railroad cars, and the wagon side was then released to dump the beets into the car below. Some wagons even had tilting floors.

To Isabel Wyckoff, even though Cyrus had been their best for many years, the railroad offered nothing more than the salaries her husband had already earned, plus a full day's pay for the day he died. Angered by such a lack of company caring, she promptly filed a $50,000 negligence suit. It was later settled out of court at a much lower figure.

FROM THE FILES OF THE PVC—the following is a collection of notes, reports, and short anecdotes gleaned from the files of the Pajaro Valley Consolidated Railroad concerning accident problems and other hazards along the right-of-way. For the most part they are self-explanatory.

Like other railroads, the PVC had their problems with "prize animals" wandering onto the right-of-way and being killed. The engineers were required to make a written report of such accidents immediately upon reaching the terminal. The railroad most often took little notice of the farmer's description of the "prize animal" and, therefore, usually paid considerably less than the sum requested.

Jan. 19th. '01

STATEMENT OF JOHN ROLAND, Engineer.

On Wednesday Jan. 16th. '01, going towards Watsonville, Cal. at about one-quarter of a mile south of Bardin's Switch, running along at a speed of about 25 miles per hour, I struck a hog weighing about 125 lbs. I whistled repeatedly, but that did not seem to disturb the hog.

(Signed) John Roland
ENGINEER

Mr. Chas. Cravas
Salinas, Cal.

Dear Sir,

We are in receipt of your letter of the 10th, inst., in regard to a hog belonging to you, being run over and killed on the line of our road, and have the following to state in relation thereto:—that we have given your claim for $25.00 damages due consideration and cannot see our way clear to allow you more than five dollars for the hog. Your cattle broke down the fence which allowed the hog to pass through onto our right-of-way, and upon statements of train-men and all in consideration, we cannot allow you more than $5.00 for the hog. Should you decide to accept same, please advise us and we will forward you our check for that amount.

Yours Truly,
(signed) W.C. Waters General Manager

July 27, 1901

Mr. J.B. Simas
Watsonville, Cal.

Dear Sir,

We are in receipt of a bill against us, from you, for $110.00 for three cows killed—two, Aug. 21, 1900—$60.00, and one on July 13, 1901—$50.00.

In regard to your claim for the two cows killed Aug. 21, 1900, would ask for full particulars as we cannot accept your bare statement that two cows, belonging to you, were killed by our train nearly a year ago, and you just presenting your claim against us for the damages claimed to have been done.

In regard to the cow claimed to have been killed by our train on July 13th last, and for which you ask to be reimbursed $50.00, we would ask you if $50.00 for a yearling calf isn't rather a high price, and did you not put the calf on our right-of-way yourself?

Yours Truly,
(signed) W.C. Waters – Gen. Mang.

Sept. 10, 1901

Mr. J.B. Simas,
Watsonville, Cal.

Dear Sir,

We enclose herewith draft and voucher for $45.00. While we do not feel that we are justified in paying you this amount, we will do so if you care to settle the matter. Considering all the value of the stock and the presumption that if the yearling had not been killed you would as yet not presented the claim for the two cows claimed to have been killed, by you over a year ago, we are of the opinion you are getting the best of the proposition, and which we are willing to grant, having in view thereby the continuance of our good relations as in the past.

Yours Truly,
(signed) W.C. Waters, Gen. Mang.

The only known grade crossing accident was at the county road crossing north of Spreckels when two women ran into the side of the Salinas passenger train. The two women were evidently engaged in conversation and did not notice until it was too late that the train, traveling parallel to their car, was about to cross the road they were on. While the car was demolished, the two women escaped with only minor injuries. Oddly enough, the driver of the car was the wife of PVC engineer Bradley. Fortunately, he was not the engineer on this train. Otherwise, he probably would have received even more ribbing from fellow engineers than he did get.

There was probably one unhappy little girl after her father received the following letter regarding vandalism from General Manager Waters:

Aug. 8, 1903

Mr. Moses Jordan,
Castroville, Cal.

Dear Sir: –

Your daughter, Sadie Jordan, threw a rock through our coach window of the P. V. C. R. R. This is a very dangerous proceeding as, if anybody had been injured, we would have had to collect damages from you, for same. We would be pleased to have you send us $5 to repair the window, and see in the future that such things do not occur, as it is a penitentiary offense.

Yours Truly,
(signed) W.C. Waters
GENERAL MANAGER

THERE WERE EXCURSIONS – the narrow gauge, being in keen competition with the Southern Pacific for traffic, readily accepted any logical proposal to operate an excursion or special train to promote good public relations. Whenever there was a special event in either Watsonville or Salinas that could not be covered by the regular scheduled train hours, a special or excursion train would be operated. When the PVC did not have enough passenger cars to handle such specials, boxcars with benches would be pressed into service.

Typical examples included extra night runs to allow lodge members to attend special meetings. The train would leave in the early evening and return late that same night or even the next morning. Whenever the Ringling Brothers circus appeared in Salinas, a roundtrip special was operated from Watsonville with a fare of $1.00 for adults and $.50 for children. Example:

February 6, 1910
Salinas *Californian*

There will be a special run of the Pajaro Valley Consolidated Railroad from Spreckels and Watsonville to Salinas every Friday and Monday evening to allow residents of the nearby communities to attend the show.

All the surrounding towns had baseball teams, which created the need for more special trains. The Watsonville games were played at the beach park, and connection was made

Mrs. Bradley's wrecked car. Photograph courtesy Ross Riley Collection

Big doings at Lake Watsonville. Photograph courtesy Pajaro Valley Historical Association

with the narrow gauge Watsonville Transportation Company to transfer passengers for the trip to the beach. A former PVC employee reports that when the Watsonville narrow gauge electric had insufficient cars, they were borrowed from the PVC.

The following letter is an example of how far the railroad went to help organizations and generate additional business:

W.J. Pierson Esq.
Agent, Salinas
Dear Sir,
Replying to your telegram of this date: Mr. Waters will give the baseball club the proceeds of the round trip tickets sold at Salinas over $75.00 (seventy-five dollars) on next Sunday's Excursion. All fares collected on the train will go to the P. V. C. R. R. in addition to the above $75.00.
I will have 150 special excursion tickets printed and send them to you on Saturday morning. You will please sell these tickets at the train on Sunday morning.

Yours Truly,
(signed) P.W. Morse

There were two annual events held in Watsonville that called for special excursion trains to handle the large crowds of people from the surrounding cities. One was the Fourth of July celebration, and the other was the Apple Show.

During the summer the Pajaro River was dammed up to form a lake, referred to as Lake Watsonville. For the Fourth of July lights were strung up along the lake shore, and a floating bandstand was set up. There was keen competition among boat owners for prizes, and boats of all designs and sizes were entered. It was not uncommon for people to fall into the shallow lake, and on one occasion the Queen's barge sank.

In 1909 Watsonville was the largest apple producing area in the world, shipping over 4,000 carloads of apples and cider. In that year a committee was formed to organize the Annual Apple Show. The show was a five-day event, with the slogan "An Apple Show Where Apples Grow." The event included a box-making contest, an apple-picking contest, band concerts, parades, and a Mardi Gras type of street dance. The show drew 30,000 people from throughout the state. After four years the show got so big that it was moved to San Francisco, where it was combined with a statewide agricultural show.

Change, Growth, and Success

All during the Glory Years, while the PVC was expanding via its many branches, and the Pacific Coast Steamship Company was developing a very lucrative seagoing business, the big kid down the block, the Southern Pacific, had not been sitting idle. In 1886, SP management had made the decision to turn its Gilroy to Soledad branch into a San Francisco to Los Angeles coastal mainline. Fifteen years later, on March 31, 1901, the line began temporary operations via a rather circuitous inland route through Santa Barbara and Saugus. A short time later, on March 20, 1904, the SP Coast Division was completed as originally planned along the ocean, via Santa Barbara and Burbank, and twelve- to fourteen-hour passenger train service began over the line.

The completion of the SP coast route meant the beginning of many good and not so good things for the people in the Salinas-Watsonville area. First of all, Watsonville (Pajaro, later Watsonville Junction) became a division point for the SP because of its close proximity to the Santa Cruz branch, the Hollister branch, the Monterey branch, and independent operations and customers like the San Juan Pacific Railway and the Granite Rock operations at Logan. Second, the railroad's completion meant immediate access to new markets and products, previously inaccessible, by helping to strengthen the links between the Pacific Northwest, Southern California, and many points east. Third, with good connections to most freight-generating areas up and down the coast, it helped to establish competitive freight rates between the SP and the Pacific Coast Steamship Company, which benefited their customers. Last, because the completion of the coast route brought with it a change in transportation technology, many stage, wagon, and barge freight lines, operating antiquated equipment, were forced out of business.

For the Pacific Coast Steamship Company, the twelve- to fourteen-hour passenger schedule offered by the SP meant the end of its passenger service in 1907. With regard to freight, however, the new service opened up more avenues of joint interchange and provided much additional business.

During this time of SP accomplishments, the PVC continued to grow and expand, reaching the pinnacle of its success. A tenth locomotive was added to the roster, a used 2-4-4T, No.51 from the Florence & Cripple Creek Railroad in Colorado. It was put into service on the Salinas branch. In addition, all of the company's other locomotives were converted from coal to fuel oil by the Holland Company in 1908. The passenger roster was also filled out to include four first-class coaches, two second-class coaches, three baggage-passenger combines, and an express car. The passenger mixed schedule was expanded to three trains a day each way between Watsonville and Spreckels, with two additional trains operating between Spreckels and Moss Landing during peak traffic times. The following is an example of the schedule for both employees and passengers during the early 1900s.

**PAJARO VALLEY
CONSOLIDATED RAILROAD COMPANY**

Spreckels, Cal., Sept. 29, 1902

(Employee Timetable)

ARRIVAL AND DEPARTURE OF TRAINS

TRAIN NO. 1:   J.A. Huff, Conductor; J. Roland, Engineer;

Leaves Watsonville daily, except Sundays, at 8 A.M. and 1:15 P.M.

Leaves Spreckels daily, except Sundays, at 10 A.M., and 4 P.M.

Train #1 will pass train #3 at Moss Landing between 8 and 9 A.M., and between 4:30 and 6 P.M.

Train #1 must look out for train #2 while passing through Cooper Ranch

TRAIN NO. 2:   C.M. Tucker, Conductor; C.E. Bradley, Engineer;

Leaves Spreckels daily, except Sundays, at 6 A.M., and 12 M.

Arrives at Spreckels before train #1 leaves in the morning and afternoon.

Train #2 to look out for train #1 at Cooper Ranch.

TRAIN NO. 3:   J.J. Maher, Conductor; T.J. Morehead, Engineer;

Leaves Spreckels daily, except Sundays, at 6:30 A.M., passing train #1 at Moss Landing, arriving at Watsonville at 9:20 A.M.

Returning, leaves Watsonville at 3:30 P.M., passing train #1 at Moss Landing, arrives at Spreckels not later than 7 P.M.

In effect Sept. 29, 1902   *W.C. WATERS, Gen. Mgr.*

(Approximate Schedule)*						
Southbound	Mi.	No. 1	No. 2	2-No. 1	2-No. 2	No. 3
Watsonville...	0.0	8:00AM	– – –	1:15PM	– – –	3:30PM
Moss Landing .	9.8	8:45AM	8:30AM	2:00PM	1:45PM	5:30PM
Cooper Ranch .	15.1	8:55AM	8:45AM	2:10PM	2:00PM	5:50PM
Spreckels	27.2	9:45AM	9:50AM	3:00PM	3:15PM	7:00PM

Northbound	Mi.	No. 2	No. 3	No. 1	2-No. 2	2-No. 1
Spreckels	0.0	6:00AM	6:30AM	10:00AM	12:00PM	4:00PM
Cooper Ranch .	12.1	7:00AM	8:00AM	11:10AM	1:00PM	5:00PM
Moss Landing .	17.4	7:15AM	8:30AM	11:30AM	1:15PM	5:15PM
Watsonville...	27.2	– – –	9:15AM	1:00PM	– – –	6:30PM

*Does not include any of the 27 flag stops between Watsonville and Spreckels.

Finally, two long spurs, both requiring extensive bridge work, were laid down to open up new loading areas for local farmers. One was at Struve Station, two miles south of Moss Landing, where a 250-foot trestle was built west across the Salinas River leading into a 1,834-foot spur. The other was at Cassin, five miles from Watsonville, where a 160-foot bridge across the Pajaro River led to a 1,361-foot spur and then a second 2,900-foot spur that doubled back along the opposite side of the river toward Watsonville.

Thus, during the Glory Years Claus Spreckels's narrow gauge, which had originally started out as an extension of his Western Beet Sugar factory at Watsonville, became a quality third-class railroad, making well over $100,000 a year for many years in succession. While the Pajaro Valley Consolidated Railroad was a small operation when compared to Claus Spreckels's larger concerns, it definitely made a profit for him.

Claus Spreckels himself lived to see it all happen, then passed the reins of power to his sons. His son John became president of the railroad, and his son Adolph, vice-president. The youngest of the sons, Rudolph, eventually took over the family's larger enterprises. On December 26th, 1908, Claus Spreckels passed away at the age of eighty, leaving his mark forever on the history of Steinbeck Country, the state of California, and the United States.

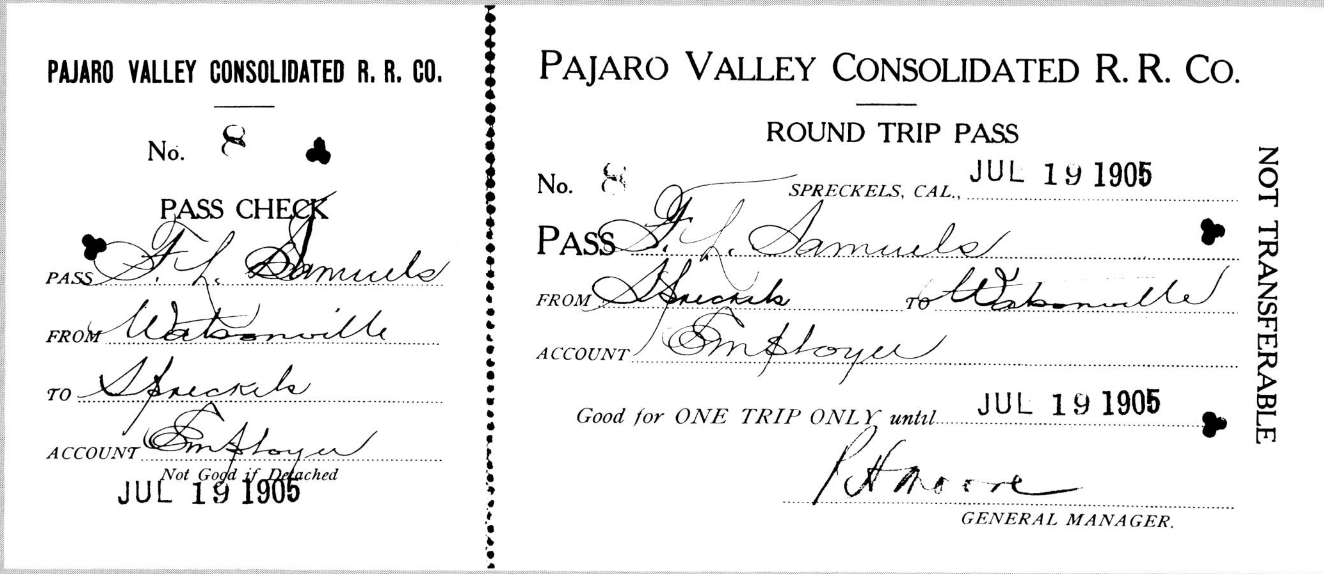

PAJARO VALLEY CONSOLIDATED R. R. CO.

No. 8 ♣

PASS CHECK

PASS *F. L. Samuels*

FROM *Watsonville*

TO *Spreckels*

ACCOUNT *Employee*

Not Good if Detached

JUL 19 1905

PAJARO VALLEY CONSOLIDATED R. R. CO.

ROUND TRIP PASS

JUL 19 1905

No. 8

SPRECKELS, CAL.,

PASS *F. L. Samuels*

FROM *Spreckels* TO *Watsonville*

ACCOUNT *Employee*

Good for ONE TRIP ONLY until JUL 19 1905

R. H. Moore

GENERAL MANAGER.

NOT TRANSFERABLE

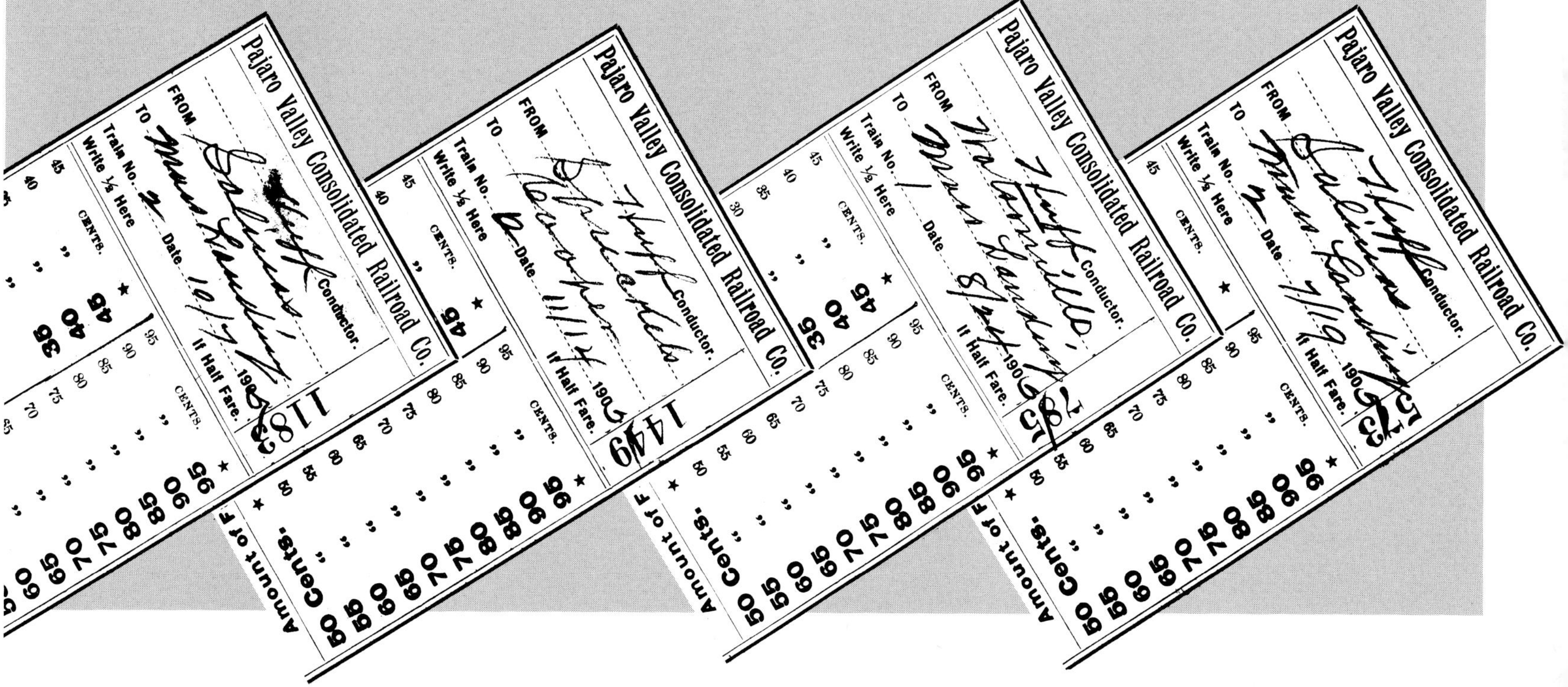

Typical of the many steam tractors used in Steinbeck Country and across the nation is the one shown above.
Photograph courtesy Miss Rose Rhyner, Spreckels Sugar Company Collection

These tilting wagons, pictured in November of 1907, were designed especially for hauling sugar beets by the area farmers and were used for many years thereafter. Photograph courtesy Miss Rose Rhyner, Spreckels Sugar Company Collection

The beet wagon is driven into position on the dumping platform at Ranch No. 1, the wagon tilts sideways, and the beets are unloaded. Photograph courtesy Amstar, Spreckels Collection

Then the mules that were used to unload are unleashed from the lines, and the wagon is driven away.

The beet cars have been unloaded at the dump, and one of the PVC Moguls now moves them out of the Spreckels Sugar factory. Photograph courtesy Ted Wurm, Gilbert Kniess Collection

Steam donkeys running on standard gauge track unload the narrow gauge cars at the factory. Photograph courtesy Monterey County Historical Society

Right-of-way spraying equipment lines the spur at Spreckels depot. Photograph courtesy Amstar, Spreckels Collection

In these two views, the right-of-way is being sprayed rather than being burned with the weed burner. Photographs courtesy Amstar, Spreckels Collection

Typical of right-of-way maintenance and bridge repair were these two scenes at the PVC Pajaro River bridge crossing near Watsonville. Photographs courtesy Miss Rose Rhyner, Spreckels Sugar Company Collection

Engine No. 1 and two Moguls are seen at the Spreckels engine house. Photograph courtesy Bob Willey Collection

The PVC Spreckels engine house seems small when compared to the factory buildings behind it. Photograph courtesy Amstar, Spreckels Collection

A Pajaro Valley Consolidated combine and two coaches sit ready for use at Spreckels. Photograph courtesy Vernon Sappers Collection

PVC coach No. 6 is pictured at Spreckels. Photograph courtesy Vernon Sappers Collection

Presumed to be the original Spreckels depot, this wooden structure is, as of this view, a barber shop. Photograph courtesy Amstar, Spreckels Collection

Spreckels Sugar Company factory during the off season. Photograph courtesy Amstar, Spreckels Collection

These two views show the PVC right-of-way, first along the Salinas River near its mouth, then a little farther north near the station point of Beach. Photographs courtesy Amstar, Spreckels Collection

Originally Western Beet Sugar Company No. 1, PVC No. 8 sits idle at Spreckels. Photograph courtesy University of California, Berkeley, Bancroft Library

The PVC narrow gauge was not the only way beets were shipped to Spreckels by train. Here, beets are loaded aboard SP standard gauge cars near King City, California. Photograph courtesy Amstar, Spreckels Collection

In this picture yet another local railroad is involved in the shipment of beets to Spreckels. At the station point of Canfield in the San Juan Valley beets are loaded aboard San Juan Pacific standard gauge cars. Photograph courtesy Stanford University Library

Children will probably continue to be photographed in the cab of a locomotive for as long as there are railroads on which to run them. So it was for William and Rose Rhyner in the early 1900s, posing in the gangway of the second No. 1 at Spreckels. Photograph courtesy Monterey County Historical Society

V / WHERE ONCE THERE WAS A FLEETING WISP OF GLORY

FOR THE PAJARO VALLEY CONSOLIDATED RAILROAD the final years of operation, while not glorious, were substantial. From 1915 until 1920 the line saw continued profitable gross revenues in the $75,000 to $100,000 range. Because it was running fewer but longer trains, the PVC stayed in the black. The equipment was in good shape, the line was in excellent condition, and the operations kept forty-five full-time employees busy.

In 1915, the PVC had its best year in terms of operating earnings – $15,328 in gross passenger revenues and $73,855 in gross freight revenues. In 1917, the railroad handled its highest tonnage ever – over 11,600 carloads of freight, which represented 174,480 tons of product and produce. In 1919, the narrow gauge saw its largest ridership – 158,871 passengers. Finally, in 1920, the PVC recorded its most successful operating year. Before it was over, the railroad had grossed $135,218, receiving $25,662 in passenger fares, $87,451 in freight earnings, and $22,105 in mail, express, communications, and warehousing revenues.

Jerry McCabe, longtime Watsonville resident and fireman and engineer for the SP for over fifty years, remembers the PVC and the beginning of 1921 very well. He had just finished working as an engineer and fireman for the famed San Vicente Lumber Company north of Santa Cruz. Now they were closed and he was looking for a job. "I had several friends working for the P-Vine and they were always after me to come on over and apply as the road was in good shape and had a fine future. . . . I turned them down however, and went to work for the Southern Pacific because they offered more money. . . . Who would have believed that just seven years later it would be gone."

Typical of the latter-day steam-powered freight train hauling beets in the Salinas Valley is this one, pictured near Sargent, California. Photograph by Fred C. Stoes

2-6-0 No. 7 rotates on the Watsonville turntable during the 1920s. Note that the Western Beet Sugar Company factory is gone. Photograph courtesy William Harry Collection

2-6-2T No. 9 takes on water at Spreckels during lunchtime so the afternoon schedule can be adhered to. Photograph courtesy University of California, Berkeley, Bancroft Library

PVC No. 10 is about to leave Salinas with the afternoon Spreckels local. Photograph courtesy University of California, Berkeley, Bancroft Library

November 4, 1919. The afternoon mixed for Spreckels from Watsonville has just made the stop at Moss Landing.
Photograph courtesy University of California, Berkeley, Bancroft Library

Decline and Abandonment

World War I was responsible for extending the life of the narrow gauge freight and passenger business into the early 1920s while at the same time hastening the development of the internal combustion engine, which would bring about the PVC's demise. As transportation technology began to change from horse- and steam-powered forms of conveyance to those powered by the internal combustion engine, many of the smaller railroads and larger company branch lines would disappear. The end of the Pajaro Valley Consolidated came gradually because it controlled the hauling of sugar beets and most of the local freight produced by the sugar factory.

Naturally, the first traffic to decline was that over which Pajaro Valley Consolidated had no control. This included local shipments along the mainline, express, passengers, and of prime importance, intercarrier freight shipments via the oceangoing connections at Moss Landing.

It is lost to history as to which declined first, the farm and produce rail shipments to Moss Landing or the availability of ships to carry freight to San Francisco. In any case, the gradual change by local farmers and cattle ranchers to truck, and the increased use of the Southern Pacific mainline between San Francisco and Los Angeles, because of better service and faster trains, marked the beginning of the end for coastal steamships. The first to go were the small steamers that carried general cargo up and down the coast to ports such as Monterey, Santa Cruz, and Moss Landing. Next were the larger concerns like the Pacific Coast Steamship Company, which cut back operations in 1915 when they sold out to the Pacific–Alaska Navigation Company. Although the Pacific–Alaska Navigation Company carried on under the PCSS Co. name, dockings at Moss Landing became less frequent. Sometime during the 1920s they ceased altogether. The last ships to call at the port of Moss Landing were the steam lumber schooners in 1933, which used to off-load lumber at the Sandholt Yards nearby.

Through the years several freight cars had been retired, and in 1918 the first rolling stock was removed from the property when five flatcars and engine No.1 were sold for scrap. The once-proud little Baldwin 2-4-2T, which had given up its long-time passenger duties in 1915 to No.10 on the Salinas branch, was sold for the sum of only $870.16. The first abandonment of track took place in September of 1920 when 3.04 miles of line and sidings were abandoned and removed on the Alisal branch. This trackage had served a large cattle feed lot at the end of the branch, as well as the Alisal picnic grounds.

On July 14, 1921, the articles of incorporation were amended to permit the carrying of passengers and property by bus, stage, or automobile upon the highway. Soon after, a bus was purchased to handle some of the Salinas branch traffic. As the mainline passenger service between Spreckels and Watsonville was handled by mixed trains, the bus only operated in the area served by the Salinas branch.

In 1922, sixty-eight of the small four-wheel dump cars were sold for $70.00 each and shipped to an unknown operation in the Philippines. At one time the railroad had over 105 of these small cars, some of which were built in the railroad's shops. For years they had been used only around the factory to haul residual to the river levees; they had been replaced for pulp service by larger volume gondolas.

Like other faltering railroads of the time, the Pajaro Valley Consolidated had no control over its passenger traffic. The only true passenger trains operating over the line by the 1920s were on the Salinas branch, since the Spreckels to Watsonville mixed had been cut to just seasonal operations during peak times. By 1925 the eight daily round trips being made between Spreckels and Salinas had been cut to just two: trains No. 1 and 2 during the morning peak, and trains No. 13 and 14 in the evening. The other six remaining round trips had been relegated to the bus. The morning trains and one bus run were not operated on Sunday, while a late bus was put on at night.

The end of passenger train service on the Salinas branch took place on Tuesday, November 24, 1925. The following morning the bus schedule was increased to seven round trips daily. From that time on, the only passenger trains operating, except for the seasonal mixed train on the mainline, were

It has been some time since the last passenger train left Salinas for Spreckels. Still, the old depot presents a fine place to while away the hours on a long afternoon. Photograph by Benny Romano

The once-active Spreckels engine house is now a storage area for miscellaneous equipment. Photograph courtesy Amstar, Spreckels Collection

October 12, 1931. PVC No. 10, built by Schenectady Locomotive Works, sits on the dead track, never again to run under steam. Photograph by Jack Sherwood from Fred C. Stoes Collection

In these two views, ex-PVC flatcars now serve another purpose at Moss Landing. Photographs courtesy Fred C. Stoes Collection

September 23, 1930. The end of the Pajaro Valley Consolidated is at hand. In this last motive power picture the company's engines have literally been turned out to pasture. Photograph courtesy University of California, Berkeley, Bancroft Library

excursion trains for special events.

It is not known when the last revenue run was made on the railroad. The 1927 campaign was the last for the PVC, which means that the trains would have been operating until the spring of 1928. The Moody *Manual of Investments: Railroads 1929* verifies this, showing a gross revenues received figure of $27,375 for the year 1928.

In June of 1928, the Pajaro Valley Consolidated petitioned the Interstate Commerce Commission for abandonment. On October 10, 1928, that abandonment was approved. On April 2, 1929, the railroad likewise petitioned the California State Public Utilities Commission and on August 1 received their approval.

On December 5, 1929, the entire road and all of its material and property holdings, valued at $1,300,000, were sold by the majority stockholder, the Spreckels Sugar Company, to the Southern Pacific for the sum of ten dollars. The sale included 40.03 miles of right-of-way and everything contained thereon, all buildings and maintenance structures, all franchise powers and immunities, 7 locomotives, 24 boxcars, 140 gon-

dola cars, 4 flatcars, 3 dismantled dump cars, 2 combination baggage and passenger cars, and 3 coaches. The Spreckels Sugar Company retained all Pajaro Valley Consolidated Railroad records and cash on hand; 2 standard gauge steam engines; all tracks within the Spreckels Sugar Factory yard, and 2 motorized buses for use between Spreckels and Salinas, California.

Disposition of the rolling stock and physical plant by the SP is unknown, except that two gondola cars and two tank cars were sold to the Nevada County Narrow Gauge Railroad for operation on the line between Colfax and Nevada City, California. Several of the box cars were purchased by farmers for storage. One car, perhaps the last to survive, rests on a ranch in Gonzales minus running gear. Whether any of the cars were ever moved to the SP narrow gauge operation in the Owens Valley is unknown. The locomotives were eventually moved out of the Spreckels yard and stored on a siding east of the factory. After six years on the dead track, the Southern Pacific in 1935 finally cut all of them up for scrap.

After the Pajaro Valley Consolidated

The abandonment of the PVC did not mean the complete end of narrow gauge railroad operations along the old right-of-way. For a number of years afterwards the wharf at Moss Landing, operating under a federal permit, was used by fishing boats to tie up to and to off-load their catches. The catches were usually transferred to six ex-PVC flatcars that had been converted into hoppers, and twenty four-wheeled smaller cars that were pulled around the narrow gauge trackage to the various canneries by a gas powered locomotive. This trackage included the old Salinas River Bridge and the PVC wye. When the operation finally concluded, shortly after the end of World War II, the six PVC flatcars were unceremoniously run off the end of the wharf into Monterey Bay.

In addition to use by the fishing boats, the wharf did serve other purposes. In 1932, Standard Oil Company of California opened a marine terminal at Moss Landing, which was served by small coastal tankers. The tankers anchored about 150 feet off the end of the wharf and pumped their cargo ashore through a hose connected to a pipeline on the wharf. The Moss Landing terminal was closed in 1956 when a pipeline was constructed from the Richmond refinery to a terminal in San Jose. After Standard Oil moved on, the wharf was still used by fishermen for a number of years until it fell into such poor condition that it had to be closed. In 1977, it was repaired and still remains in use, although it is somewhat shorter than it was in the Pacific Coast Steamship Company days.

For the most part, after the narrow gauge was taken up at Spreckels, trucks, buses, and the Southern Pacific replaced the PVC operations. For the next fifty-two years, the Spreckels Sugar Factory continued to refine sugar as it had since its beginnings in 1897. During this time, the Spreckels Sugar Company owned and operated several standard gauge steam and diesel locomotives, which they used to move gondolas and other cars around their and the Southern Pacific's adjoining yards.

On July 28, 1982, after eighty-five years of continuous operation, the Spreckels Sugar Company refined its last ton of raw sugar beets through the plant that at one time was the largest such facility in the world. Because the farmers in the local agricultural areas of the Pajaro, San Benito, and Salinas valleys had found more lucrative crops, and because sugar beets therefore had to be transported from as far away as the San Joaquin Valley for processing, the cost of shipping the beets eventually forced the plant to close. Today, the only operation still going on is the packaging of refined sugar.

During the ensuing years, following the abandonment of the PVC, the Spreckels family gradually relinquished its holdings in the Spreckels Sugar Company. Eventually, it became a part of the American Sugar Refineries, a company Claus Spreckels helped begin. Today, Amstar, as it is known, is a two-billion-dollar-a-year corporation, operating many refineries all over the United States. It, too, found its humble beginnings during the days of the Steinbeck Country Narrow Gauge, when dreamers like David Jacks, Claus Spreckels, and John Steinbeck saw the area for what it was, the lands that were both Eden and east of Eden.

Ex-SP standard gauge, No. 1085, now Spreckels Sugar Co. No. 1085, poses in the same spot where only recently the PVC narrow gauge No. 8, No. 9, and No. 10 locomotives dominated. Photograph courtesy Bob Willey Collection

Locomotive Engineer Robert Weimer and Fireman Jack Freire put No. 1085 through its paces during the early 1940s. Today the profession of railroadman at Spreckels continues in the family. John Weimer, Robert's son, has followed in his father's footsteps and now works the company's diesels. Photograph courtesy John Weimer

Ex-SP engine No. 1100, now Spreckels's second standard gauge engine, is seen running light in the yard. Photograph courtesy Guy Dunscomb Collection

The diesel age has come to Spreckels. Here, No. 1 takes a bow. Photograph courtesy Francis Guido

The year is 1937. The PVC is gone from Steinbeck Country. The Pacific Coast Steamship Company coastal passenger steamers between San Francisco and Los Angeles are no more. Now there is a new kid on the block. This Southern Pacific Golden State locomotive is seen leaving Salinas on the first 9¾-hour high speed run of the historic Daylight. Photograph by Fred C. Stoes

The new Los Angeles-bound Daylight, No. 98, has just arrived in Salinas. Photograph by Fred C. Stoes

It's late in the 1940s, and a Standard Oil Tanker is moored at the end of the Moss Landing wharf. Photograph by Fred C. Stoes

For a few days in the early 1950s there was yet another railroad operating into Spreckels. Above, a Southwest Pacific boxcar loaded with Salinas Valley lettuce blocks the Spreckels road crossing, while left, SWP extra No. 2840 pauses near the Southern Pacific Silk car, long a local landmark. The reason? A motion picture company has arrived on the scene to film John Steinbeck's East of Eden. *Ironically, the old PVC depot at Spreckels became the substitute for the original Salinas depot. Photographs by W.L. Gerow*

Two SP diesels stop momentarily in front of the Silk car just west of the factory. This was the end of the SP and the beginning of Spreckels operations. Photograph by Horace W. Fabing

Amstar-owned ex-SP gondolas, bulging with swollen sugar beets, line the house track at Salinas, waiting for the final trip to Spreckels. Today this view as seen through the camera lens and by the passengers and crew aboard the Los Angeles-bound Amtrak Coast Starlight on May 25, 1982, is no longer possible. Photograph by Bruce MacGregor

Untold numbers of Amstar gondolas line the Spreckels Sugar factory yards where once the narrow gauge reigned supreme. Now, even this scene is no more. Photograph by Rick Hamman

The scales on which millions of tons of
sugar beets have been weighed.
Photograph by Horace W. Fabing

Once the narrow gauge rails of the Pajaro Valley Consolidated followed the course of the Salinas River near its mouth. Today the railroad is no more, and the river's mouth is closed. Photograph by Horace W. Fabing

One of the few remaining traces of the Buena Vista branch, this Salinas River concrete bridge support stands strong against the flow of time. Photograph by Bruce MacGregor

Perhaps the last vestige of the Pajaro Valley Consolidated, boxcar No. 215, now a storage shed, remains intact against the elements in Gonzales, California, a short distance from Salinas. Photograph by Horace W. Fabing

Diesel No. 2 with a heavy load of sugar beets in tow is seen leaving the joint Amstar-SP transfer yard at Spreckels, bound for the factory. Photograph by Horace W. Fabing

It is early 1980, and diesel No. 3 is seen moving beet cars around the factory, as other locomotives before it have done for eighty years. Photograph by Horace W. Fabing

Spreckels-Amstar diesel No. 2 works a string of sugar beet gondolas into the factory past the site of the original Spreckels depot. Photograph by Bruce MacGregor

May 25, 1982: Weather-beaten and old, the Spreckels Sugar factory still stands stalwart and functional after over eighty years of continuous operations. Photograph by Rick Hamman

Appendix A / Locomotive & Equipment Rosters, Steinbeck Country Narrow and Standard Gauge Railroads

Pajaro Valley (Consolidated) Railroad

Road No.	Type	Date Built	Driver Diam. (in)*	Working Weight (ton)	Steam Pressure (lbs.)	Cylinder Diam./ Stroke (in)	Baldwin Builders No.
1.	2-4-2T	6/1890	37	12	130	8 × 12	10947
2.	2-4-2T	6/1890	37	12	130	8 × 12	10954
3.	2-6-0	7/1891	36 (40)	23	150	12 × 18	12054
†2.	2-6-0	5/1892	37 (40)	27	150	12 × 18	12689
4.	2-6-0	7/1897	37 (40)	26	150	13 × 18	15368
5.	2-6-0	6/1900	40	25	150	12 × 18	17806
6.	2-6-0	6/1900	40	26	150	12 × 18	17807
7.	2-6-0	6/1900	38 (40)	26½	150	12 × 18	17808
8.	2-6-2T	7/1897	41 (45)	31	160	14 × 18	15369
9.	2-6-2T	7/1896	40 (45)	33	160	14 × 18	14954
10.	2-4-4T	5/1898	42	27	160	14 × 18	‡4740

Notes:

* The original specifications to Baldwin for locomotives second No.2–No.4 and No.7–No.9 list different driver diameter dimensions than do company engineering records of 8/29/18. Therefore, the driver diameters listed above are per the engineering record, while the diameter listed in parentheses is off the original Baldwin order. Perhaps the drivers were changed at a later date to better suit the needs of the PVC, or maybe the difference is the result of measuring the wheel diameter both with and without the tire.

1. Probably sold March 1892 to L.E. White Redwood Lumber Company. (See chapter 2, page 38.)

2. Renumbered to second No.1, May 1892. A tender was ordered from Baldwin in February of 1892 to extend the locomotive range, not always used. Scrapped 1918.

3. Ordered before No.1 was sold, therefore became No.3. Scrapped 1935.

†2. Ordered as second No.2 to replace original No.2 which became second No.1. Scrapped 1935.

4. Originally ordered at the same time as locomotive No.9 on Baldwin Specification 8618, as a double ender 2-4-2T, thirty-three-ton switcher. Lettering to read Western Beet Sugar Company. Order was evidently changed to another 2-6-0 Mogul and labeled P.V.R.R., pre–Pajaro Valley Consolidated Railroad. Scrapped 1935.

5. Scrapped 1935.

6. Scrapped 1935.

7. Scrapped 1935.

8. Originally ordered as Western Beet Sugar Company locomotive *Star.* Used at Watsonville factory. Became PVC No.8 in 1914. Scrapped 1935.

9. Originally ordered as Spreckels Sugar Company locomotive. Used at Spreckels. Became PVC No.9 in 1914. Scrapped 1935.

‡10. Built by Schenectady in May of 1898 as an 0-4-4T, No.51, *Oro,* for Golden Circle Railroad, Colorado. Sold to Florence & Cripple Creek, No.51. Subsequently rebuilt as 2-4-4T; sold to PVC as No.10 in 1914. Scrapped 1935.

PASSENGER ROSTER

Road No.	Type	Manufacturer	Year Acquired	Disposition
1.	Combination-Coach	- - - -	1897	off roster 1922
2&3.	Combination-Coach	- - - -	1908	Sold to SP 1929
4.	Coach (1st Class)	Hammond Car Co.	1905	off roster 1926
5-7.	Coach (1st Class)	Hammond Car Co.	1908	Sold to SP 1929
8&9.	Coach (2nd Class)	Mahony Brothers	1909	off roster 1916

Notes:

a. The above passenger roster is correct in all respects except for the road numbers, which are assumed. As of this writing only No.1, No.4, and No.6 are verifiable.

b. It is not known whether the passenger equipment was purchased new or used.

FREIGHT CAR ROSTER

Road Number	Car Type	Operating Weight	Year Acquired	Builder
001–100	Beet Dump	2½-ton	1890	Carter Brothers
401, 405, 424, 425, 435, 489	Beet Dump	2½-ton	- - -	PVC
101–108	flat	10-ton	1890	Carter Brothers
109–124	flat	15-ton	1891	Carter Brothers
125–199	Gondola	15-ton	1897	J.S. Hammond Car Co.
301–317 (3) Unknown	Gondola	15-ton	1894	J.S. Hammond Car Co.
318–356, 200	Gondola	15-ton	1900	J.S. Hammond Car Co.
(6) ex-flats	Gondola	15-ton	1897	J.S. Hammond Car Co./PVC
201–206	Box	10-ton	1890	Carter Brothers
207–216	Box	15-ton	1894	J.S. Hammond Car Co.
217–226	Box	15-ton	1900	J.S. Hammond Car Co.
(4) ex-flats	Tank	10-ton	1910	Carter Brothers/PVC
(1) ex-flat	Service	10-ton	1908	Carter Brothers/PVC
(2) Unknown	Caboose	10-ton	1890	Carter Brothers

Note:

a. All freight equipment was ordered new except that which was modified by the PVC.

Monterey & Salinas Valley Railroad
LOCOMOTIVE ROSTER

Road No.	Engine Name	Type	Year Built	Driver Diam. (in)	Working Weight (ton)	Cylinder Bore & Stroke (in)	Baldwin Builders No.
1.	C.S. Abbott	2-6-0	1874	40	18	12 × 16	3625
2.	Monterey	4-4-0	1875	43	22	12 × 16	3682

Notes:

1. Sold 1879, to Nevada Central Railway, became No.3, *Anson P. Stokes*; sold to Utah Eastern Railroad as No.3.

2. Sold 1879, to Nevada Central Railway, became No.4, *David B. Hatch.* Scrapped 1937.

Salinas Railway
LOCOMOTIVE ROSTER

Road No.	Type	Date Built	Baldwin Builders No.
1.	0-4-2T	10/1897	15555
2.	2-4-2T	12/1887	8955

Notes:

1. Vaulclain Compound, Steam Dummy type, sold to Corry Brothers & Adler, then to Utah Construction. Abandoned 1912 at Mackay Dam, Utah.

2. Former Park & Cliff House No.3, Ferris & Cliff House No.3. Salinas Railway sold it to Glyn & Peterson as No.2, and they sold it to E.L. White Lumber Co., Point Arena.

Spreckels Sugar Company Standard Gauge Locomotives
STEAM

Road No.	Type	Year Built	Driver Diam. (in)	Working Weight (lbs)	Steam Pressure (lbs)	Cylinder Diam./ Stroke (in)	Baldwin Builders No.
1085	0-6-0	1901	57	130,000	180	19 × 26	19486
1100	0-6-0	1902	57	130,000	180	19 × 26	20939

Notes:

1085 Originally built for the Southern Pacific as 1085, sold to Spreckels Sugar Company July 7, 1930. Scrapped October 10, 1951.

1100 Originally built for the Southern Pacific as 1100, sold to Spreckels Sugar Company July 7, 1930. Scrapped April 1947.

DIESEL

Road No.	Amstar No.	Horsepower	Working Weight	Date Built	General Electric Builders Number
1.	- - -	400	65-ton	4/1946	28470
2.	5949	400	65-ton	6/1951	30961
3.	5950	150	25-ton	7/1942	15708

Notes:

1. Transferred to Chandler, Arizona, circa 1970.

2. Active (uncertain future).

3. Transferred from Spreckels Woodland, California facility. Currently active.

Pajaro Valley Consolidated Railroad Mainline Company Stations
SPRECKELS TO WATSONVILLE
September 17, 1919

Miles From Spreckels	STATION	Miles From Watsonville	Equipment Available	Additional Trackage	Freight Car Capacity
0.0	Spreckels	27.2	R,S,#,G,	- - -	- - -
1.7	Watsonville Junc.	25.5	#,	- - -	- - -
1.8	Nacional	25.4		Spur	16
3.6	Tucker	23.6	#,G,	Siding	18
5.1	Clausen	22.1	#,G,	Siding	33
6.2	H. Bardin	21.0		Siding	9
6.5	Porter	20.7		Spur	9
7.5	C. Bardin	19.7	#,	Siding	63
	(Passing track)			- - -	48
	(Beet Loading)			Siding	19
8.2	Blanco	19.0	#,	Siding	16
9.2	Vierra	18.0		Siding	16
10.0	Dee	17.2	#,	Siding	12
12.1	Cooper	15.1	#,	Siding	24
12.8	Moro Cojo	14.4		Spur	8
13.3	Mack	13.9		Siding	20
14.1	Struve	13.7		Wye	32
14.8	Ranch	12.4	#,G,	Siding	37
15.6	Warnock	11.6		Spur	8
16.3	Thompson	11.0		Spur	2

Miles From Spreckels	STATION	Miles From Watsonville	Equipment Available	Additional Trackage	Freight Car Capacity
17.4	Moss Landing	9.8	S,#,	Wye	42
	(West Spur)			- - -	16
	(East Spur)			- - -	22
20.5	Beach	6.7		Spur	5
21.2	Tuttle	6.0		Spur	24
21.6	Jensen	5.6	#,G,	Siding	25
21.8	Gravel Pit No. 1	5.4		Spur	32
22.8	Cassin	4.9	#,	Spur	24
23.0	Williamson	4.2		Spur	11
23.7	Thurwachter	3.5		Spur	16
23.8	McGowan No. 2	3.4		Spur	10
24.2	Trafton	3.0	#,	Siding	20
	(Spur)			- - -	10
25.4	McGowan No. 1	1.8		Spur	8
25.6	Pajaro	1.6		Spur	7
26.2	Peterson	1.0		Spur	8
27.2	Watsonville Terminal	0.0	R,S,#,G,	Hse. Track	7

Notes: Car capacity at Cassin does not include bridge. Car capacity at Armstrong does not include light track off our right-of-way. Car capacities at Gravel Pit No. 1, Gravel Pit No. 2, Quarry, and Alisal do not include portable track. Car capacities at Struve and Moss Landing wyes include both legs of wyes. Car capacity at Moss Landing includes nothing beyond scales. Dashes indicate unspecified information.

Pajaro Valley Consolidated Railroad Branch Line Company Stations

SALINAS BRANCH
SPRECKELS JUNCTION TO SALINAS

Miles From Spreckels	STATION	Miles From Watsonville	Equipment Available	Additional Trackage	Freight Car Capacity
0.0	Spreckels	27.2	R,S,#,G,	- - -	- - -
1.7	Watsonville Junc.	25.5	# ,	- - -	- - -
2.5	Spreckels Junc.	26.3		- - -	- - -
3.0	Highway	26.8		Spur	5
3.6	Jeffery	27.5		Spur	9
4.2	Tynan	28.0		Spur	9
4.7	Salinas Terminal	28.5	# ,	Siding	5
	(House Track)			- - -	10

ALISAL BRANCH
WATSONVILLE JUNCTION TO RANCH #6

Miles From Spreckels	STATION	Miles From Watsonville	Equipment Available	Additional Trackage	Freight Car Capacity
0.0	Spreckels	27.2	R,S,#,G,	- - -	- - -
1.7	Watsonville Junc.	25.5	# ,	- - -	- - -
2.5	Spreckels Junc.	26.3		- - -	- - -
4.6	Carr	28.4		Siding	12
6.8	Quarry	30.6		Spur	15
7.8	Alisal	31.6		Siding	51
7.9	Ranch #6 Terminal	32.3		Siding	5

BUENA VISTA BRANCH
SPRECKELS TO BUENA VISTA

Miles From Spreckels	STATION	Miles From Watsonville	Equipment Available	Additional Trackage	Freight Car Capacity
0.0	Spreckels	27.2	R,S,#,G,	- - -	- - -
0.9	Corey	28.1		Spur	5
1.4	Armstrong	28.6		Spur	19
2.1	Hill	29.3		Spur	4
2.8	Laymon	30.0		Spur	12
4.0	Seegeiken	31.2		Siding	14
4.3	Agenda	31.5		Spur)	66
4.6	Thygisen	31.8		Spur)	
4.8	Gravel Pit #2	32.0		Spur	36
6.0	Buena Vista Terminal	33.2		Spur	18

All car capacities based on length of freight cars.

Beet Car = 30'-5"
Box Car = 30'-5"
Coach   = 45'-0"

\# = Telephone Box
G = Telephone Box Grounded
R = Register Station
S = Track Scales

Appendix B

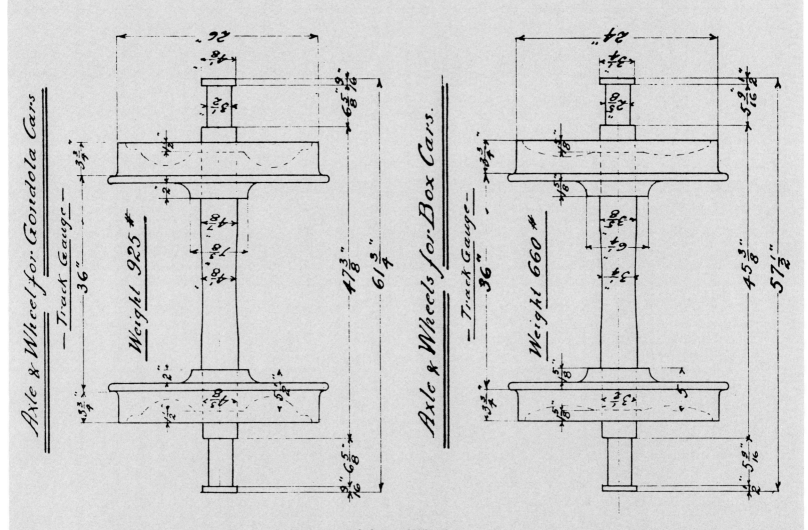

Axles and Wheels

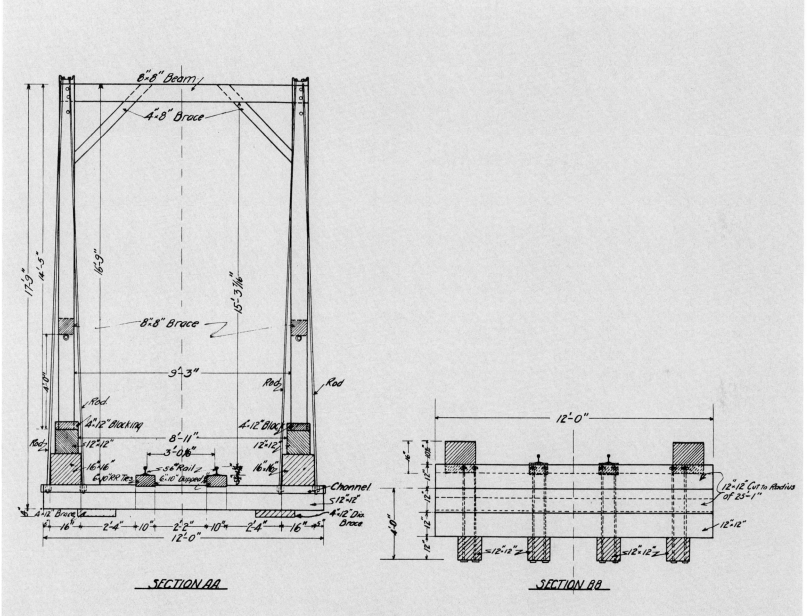

Turntable Front View

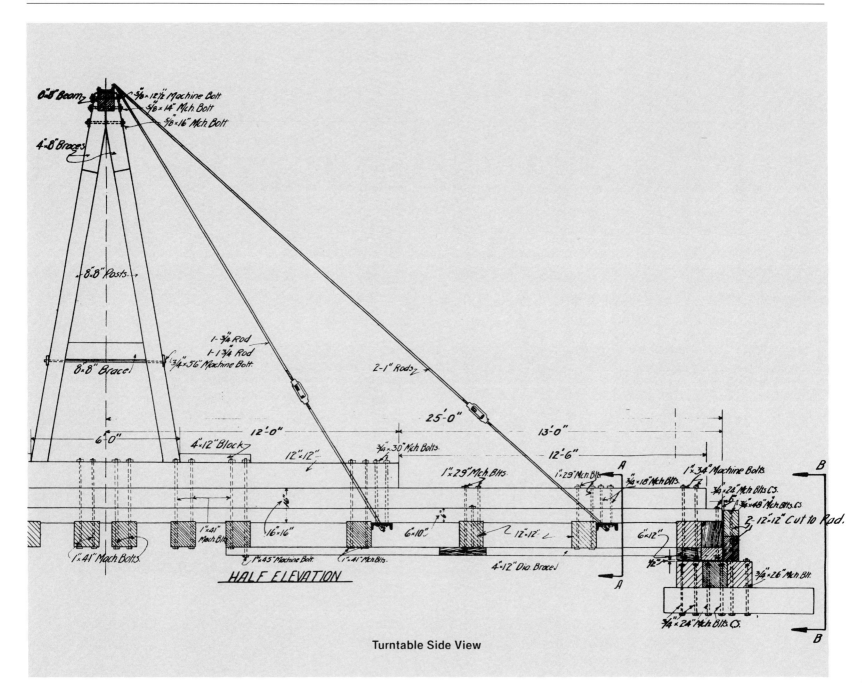

Turntable Side View

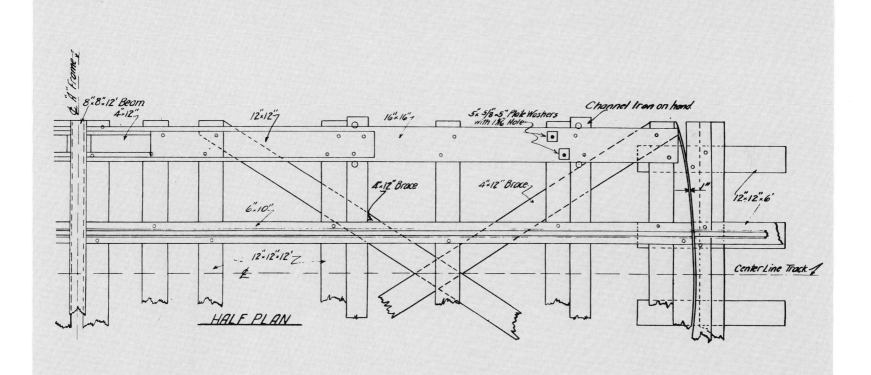

HALF PLAN

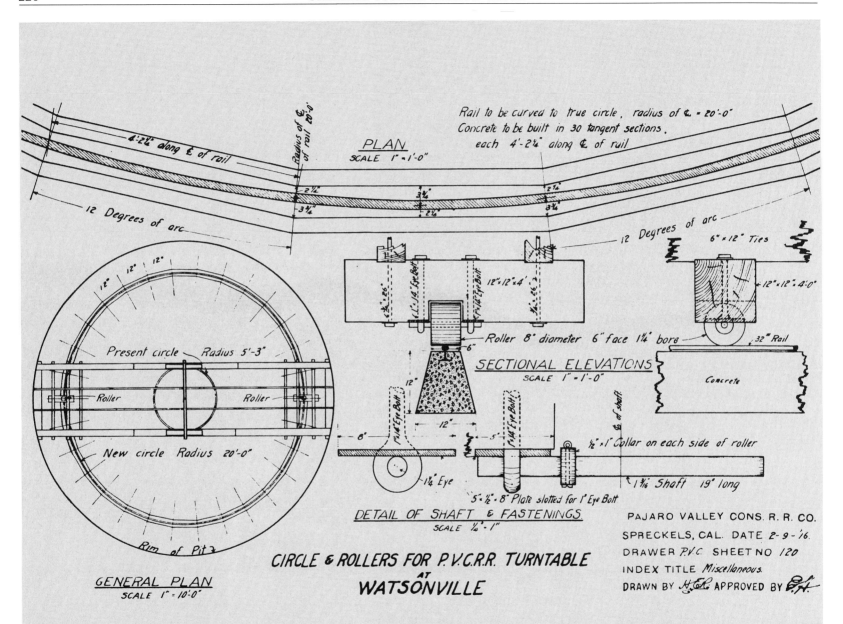

Turntable Circle

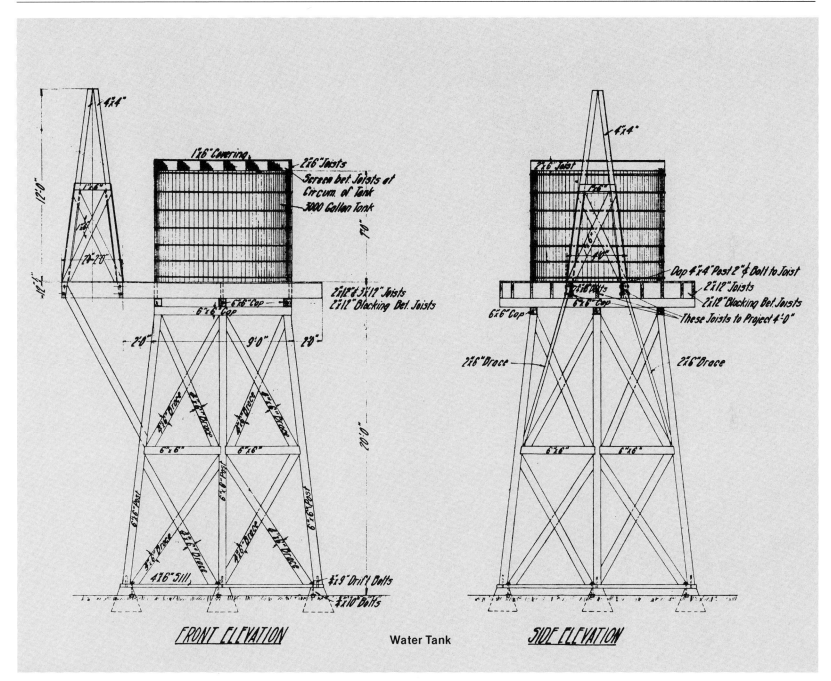

FRONT ELEVATION   Water Tank   SIDE ELEVATION

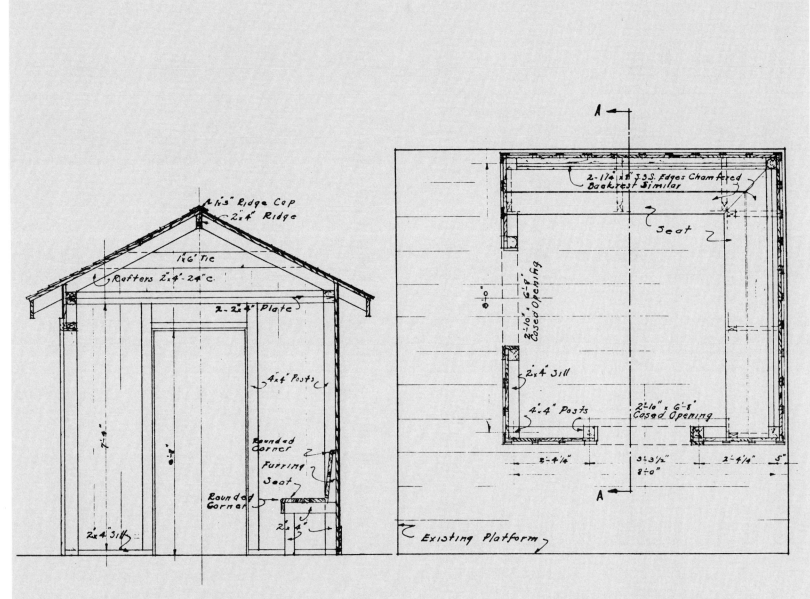

SECTION A-A   **Depot: Moss Landing**   FLOOR PLAN

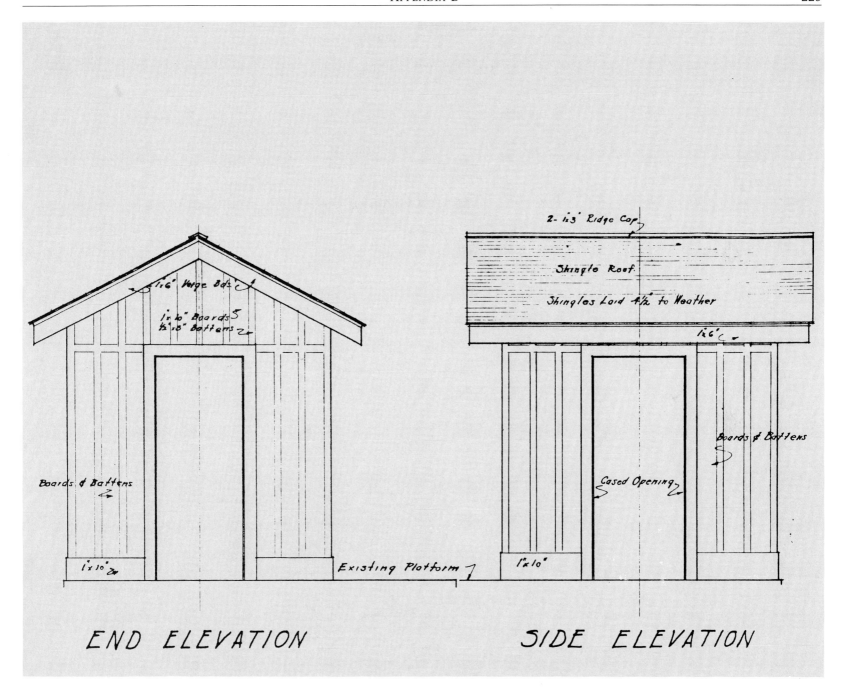

END ELEVATION   SIDE ELEVATION

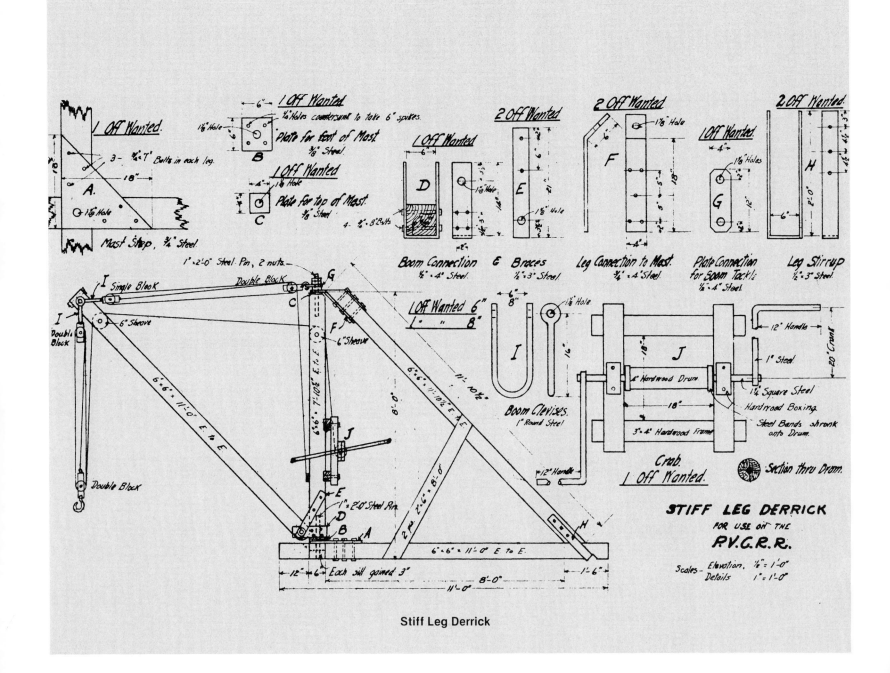

Stiff Leg Derrick

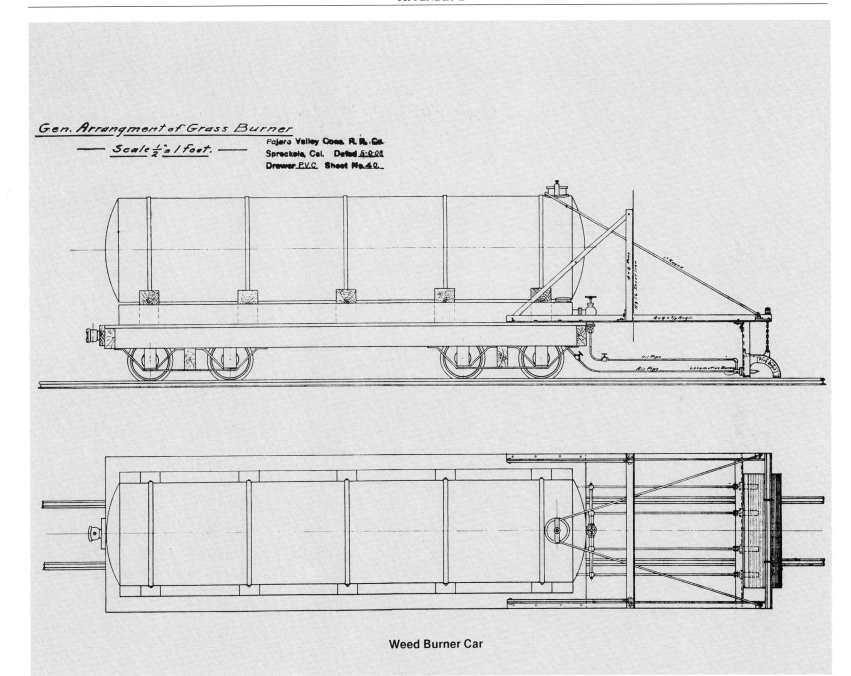

Gen. Arrangment of Grass Burner

Scale ½ = 1 foot.

Pajaro Valley Cons. R. R. Co.
Spreckels, Cal.   Dated 5-9-06
Drawer P.V.C   Sheet No. 40

Weed Burner Car

BIBLIOGRAPHY

Newspapers:

The Gilroy *Advocate,* the Gilroy *Dispatch,* the Salinas *Californian,* the San Francisco *Call* (J.D. Spreckels – Publisher), the Santa Cruz *Sentinel,* the Spreckels *Courier,* the Spreckels *Enterprise,* the Watsonville *Pajaronian.*

Magazine & Newspaper Articles:

Fabing, Horace W., "The Watsonville Transportation Company," *Western Railroader* magazine No. 322, November 1966.

Fabing, Horace W., "The Pajaro Valley Consolidated Railroad," *Western Railroader* magazine No. 489, July 1981.

Finley, James E., "A Small Brick Station," *Model Railroader* magazine Parts 1 & 2, November–December 1966.

Mann, David, "The History of Moss Landing," *Game and Gossip* magazine, January 1, 1972.

Masters, Walter, "Pajaro Valley Portrait," *Narrow Gauge and Short Line Gazette* magazine, May 1977.

Pryor, Alton, "Moss Landing, the Island was Payment to Settle a $1,500 Debt," Salinas *Californian* newspaper, June 15, 1963.

Vera, Dorothy, "May Day – Some of the Happiest were in Salinas," Salinas *Californian* newspaper, April 28, 1962.

Vera, Dorothy, "A Little Seaport that Grew and Grew," Salinas *Californian* newspaper, June 15, 1963.

Vera, Dorothy, "Take A Ride on the Spreckels Dinky Line," Salinas *Californian* newspaper, November 18, 1972.

"That Was Watsonville 50 Years Ago," Watsonville *Pajaronian* newspaper, April 2, 1962.

"That Was Watsonville 75 Years Ago," Watsonville *Pajaronian* newspaper, May 12, 1962.

Periodicals:

Monthly Catalog of Public Documents, November 1928; *I.C.C. Statistics on Railways In the United States,* 1929; *Opinions & Orders of the Railroad Commission of California,* 5/2/29 to 11/6/29, page 909.

Public Records:

I.C.C. Decision (Finance) #3401, Pajaro Valley Consolidated Railroad Abandonment, October 10, 1928; California Railroad Commission Decision #21426, Pajaro Valley Consolidated Railroad Abandonment, August 1, 1929; California Railroad Commission Report, 1876-1877, The Monterey & Salinas Valley Railroad; California Railroad Commission reports, January 1, 1911 to June 30, 1912.

Miscellaneous Pamphlets, Notes, Reports, and Unpublished Theses:

Watsonville – The First Hundred Years, published by the Watsonville Chamber of Commerce, Watsonville, 1952.

Southern Pacific Historical Outline (1931), published by the Southern Pacific.

Southern Pacific Company Coast Division Employees Timetable, September 12, 1921.

Pfingst, Edward, "The Pajaro Valley Consolidated Railroad Company," 1958.

Poor's *Manual of United States Railroads*, 1875–1879, 1902, 1903, 1908, 1909, 1910, 1912, 1916, 1919, 1925, 1928, 1929.

Moody's *Manual of Railroads*, 1904, 1908, 1912.

Moody's *Manual of Investments*, Railroads, 1918, 1920, 1925, 1927, 1929.

Pajaro Valley Consolidated *Annual Report*, 1897–1900, 1903, 1908, 1912, 1918, 1920, 1923, 1926 (on file – California Public Utilities Commission).

Pajaro Valley Railroad *Annual Report*, 1890–1895 (Amstar).

Dunn, Arthur, "Monterey County, California," *Sunset* magazine, Souvenir Edition 1915 Panama–Pacific International Exposition.

California Earthquake of April 18, 1906, Report of State Earthquake Investigation Commission, 1918 (U.S.G.S. – Menlo Park).

Travelers Official Guide, May–August 1877, The National Railway Publication Co.

Magnuson, T.A., *History of the Beet Sugar Industry In California,* Historical Society of Southern California, 1918.

"Pajaro Valley Consolidated Railroad – Moss Landing," taped interview with Albert "Bert" Vierra, 1975.

"The Official Account of the Portola Expedition of 1769–1770," edited by Frederick Teggart. Academy of Pacific Coast History Publications, Volume 1, University of California, Berkeley, California, 1910.

Books:

Abbott, C.S., *Recollections of a California Pioneer,* Neale Publishing Co., 1917.

Adler, J., *Claus Spreckels, The Sugar King in Hawaii,* University of Hawaii Press, 1966.

Best, Gerald M., *Nevada County Narrow Gauge,* Howell-North, 1965.

Best, Gerald M., *Ships & Narrow Gauge Rails, The Story of the Pacific Coast Company,* Howell-North, 1964.

Dodge, R.V., *Rails of the Silver Gate,* Pacific Railway Journal, 1960.

Dunscomb, Guy L., *A Century of Southern Pacific Steam Locomotives,* self-published, 1963.

Elliot & Moore, *History of Monterey County, 1881,* San Francisco, California.

Fisher, Anne B., *The Salinas – Upside Down River,* Farrar & Rinehart, New York, 1945.

Fleming, Howard, *Narrow Gauge Railways of America, 1875,* edited and published by Grahame Hardy and Paul Darrell, 1949. Reprint.

Hamman, Rick, *California Central Coast Railways,* Pruett Publishing, Boulder, Colorado, 1980.

Kneiss, Gilbert H., *Bonanza Railroads,* Stanford University Press, Stanford, California, 1941.

The Baldwin Locomotive Works, Catalogue of Locomotives, reprinted by Kingsport Press, 1915.

Lewis, Betty, *Watsonville, Memories That Linger,* Valley Publishers, 1976.

MacGregor, Bruce, *South Pacific Coast,* Howell-North, Berkeley, California, 1968.

McNairn, Jack and MacMullen, Jerry, *Ships of the Redwood Coast,* Stanford University Press, Stanford, California.

Morison, Samuel Eliot, *The Oxford History of the American People,* Oxford University Press, 1965.

Reinstedt, Randall, *Shipwrecks and Sea Monsters of California's Central Coast,* Ghost town Publications, 1975.

Shaw, Fisher and Harlan, *Oil Lamps and Iron Ponies,* Bay Books, 1949.

Steinbeck, John, *East of Eden,* Viking Press, 1952.

Steinbeck & His Critics, University of New Mexico Press, 1957.

INDEX